The History and Spirituality of
WALSINGHAM

Elizabeth Ruth Obbard, ODC

The Canterbury Press
Norwich

Text and line drawings © Sr Elizabeth Ruth Obbard ODC, 1995

First published 1995 by The Canterbury Press Norwich
(a publishing imprint of Hymns Ancient & Modern Limited,
a registered charity)
St Mary's Works, St Mary's Plain,
Norwich, Norfolk, NR3 3BH

British Library Cataloguing in Publication Data

A catalogue record for this book is available
from the British Library

ISBN 1–85311–118–X

*Typeset by Waveney Studios
Diss, Norfolk,
and printed in Great Britain by
Bell & Bain Ltd, Glasgow*

Other publications by Sr Elizabeth Ruth Obbard include:
Lamps of Fire, daily readings with St John of the Cross (DLT 1984);
Magnificat the Journey and the Song (DLT 1986); *La Madre*,
the Life and Spirituality of St Teresa of Avila (St Paul 1994);
Introducing Julian, Woman of Norwich (New City 1995).
She has also contributed to various books and periodicals and
written and illustrated some books for children.

Front cover photograph of Priory ruins by Louis Quail.

This book is dedicated to all
who love Walsingham
and come on pilgrimage to
the village and shrine.

It is also for the religious communities
whose members live and work
in England's Nazareth,
The Marist Fathers and Sisters
The Sisters of St Margaret
The Little Sisters of Jesus
and my own Carmelite Community.

May Mary's 'Yes' re-echo in the hearts
of each one, that we may conceive
and bear Jesus for the world,
offering him to others with
joy and humility.

ACKNOWLEDGEMENTS

I would like to thank Josef Pischler MHM for
permission to quote from his own translation
of Julian of Norwich's *Revelations of Divine
Love*, and two sisters of my community,
Penelope Brophy and Corrine O'Keeffe,
for typing the manuscript.

Contents

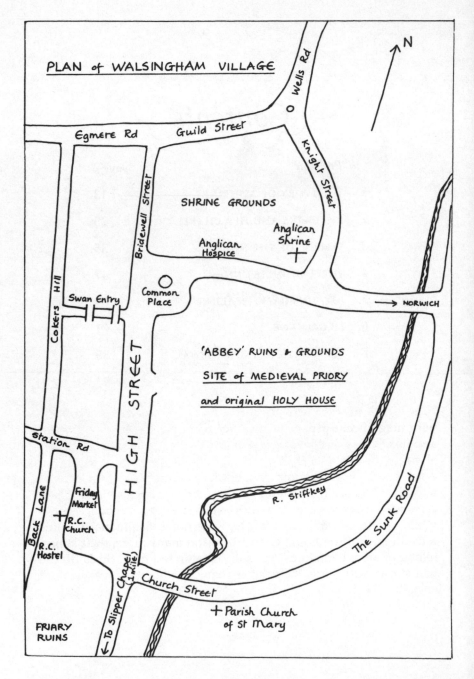

PLAN of WALSINGHAM VILLAGE

N

O Wells Rd

Knight Street

Egmere Rd   Guild Street

Bridewell Street

SHRINE GROUNDS

Anglican Hospice

Anglican Shrine ✝

Cokers Hill

Swan Entry

Common Place

→ NORWICH

HIGH STREET

'ABBEY' RUINS & GROUNDS

SITE of MEDIEVAL PRIORY

and original HOLY HOUSE

Station Rd

Back Lane

Friday Market

✝ R.C. Church

R.C. Hostel

R. Stiffkey

The Sunk Road

To Slipper Chapel (1 mile)

Church Street

✝ Parish Church of St Mary

FRIARY RUINS

Prologue

NORFOLK ... the word conjures up a picture of wide skies erupting with magnificent expanses of cloud; wide fields – fields of wheat and flax, barley and lavender as far as the eye can see; red poppies along roadsides delicately adorned with an abundance of Queen Anne's lace. This is the county of black faced sheep, of church spires and towers rising from the midst of every hamlet, grey landmarks piercing the flat horizon; churches which speak of the county's erstwhile wealth and importance. There are numerous monastic ruins too – Binham, Bromholm, Castle Acre and many more, their stones telling of an age long past yet still seeming to linger. Birds fill the hedgerows with song, their cleverly concealed nests woven around eggs, speckled, brown, blue or luminous white. Mice, voles, shrews, are still the prey of the creamy coloured barn owl which ventures forth in the dusk, while during the day hours of summer the air glistens with a haze of heat, supporting the hawk as it hovers above what the owl has missed in its nocturnal hunting.

These birds and beasts are no doubt the direct descendants of those who attracted the attention of medieval pilgrims as they passed en route to their goal – Walsingham – from all over England and even from abroad. These same fields and skies have silently witnessed throngs of palmers singing on their way to England's premier shrine of Our Lady, travelling the last lap excitedly, having stayed overnight in the priories and abbeys that are now empty ruins in a levelled land.

Norfolk villages, so sadly depleted, were once alive with the business of a thriving tourist trade; the fields produced abundant food for everyone and the hardy sheep made Norfolk rich in wool and woven cloth, attracting immigrants from the Low Countries who brought their skill and their own style of building to add variety and beauty to the landscape. In those days Norwich was the second city of the realm after London, a centre of industry with a fine cathedral served by Benedictine monks which, even today, boasts the best preserved cloisters in England.

North Norfolk, where Walsingham is situated, is slightly more undulating than South Norfolk, though even there the gentle slopes can hardly be dignified with the name of hills. Turning down a winding road which runs through one of the shallow valleys the traveller passes through the village of Houghton-le-Dale (Houghton-in-the-hole) with its parish church dedicated to St Giles, patron saint of cripples, its rood screen adorned with paintings of biblical women. And there, on the opposite side of the river Stiffkey, standing in medieval beauty beside the newly built church of Reconciliation, lies the ancient Slipper Chapel.

Looking at the Slipper Chapel in its peaceful rural setting it is hard to believe that this is England's national Roman Catholic Shrine of Our Lady. Where are the crowds? The hotels? The modern amenities? All seems silent at the place where, in pre-Reformation days, pilgrims were wont to remove their shoes before walking the last 'holy mile' into Walsingham, England's Nazareth, in their bare feet.

A mile further on, the present day pilgrim reaches Walsingham village with its narrow main street and overhanging gabled houses. Behind a large medieval gatehouse at the top of the street lie the ruins of the Augustinian Priory (now termed the Abbey) where a solitary arch dissects the skyline. Once this was the religious establishment that housed the replica of the home at Nazareth with its precious image of Our Lady of Walsingham. Turning by the village pump one sees the Anglican shrine church, completed in 1938 and containing a new holy house. Opposite is the 'knight's gate', marking the spot where it is said that in 1314 Sir Ralph Boutetourt attained sanctuary in the priory precincts when persued by his enemies. Though he was armed *cap á pied* the narrow aperture miraculously opened to allow him to pass through on horseback and thus reach safety.

In outward appearance the village could remind the traveller of Hamlyn in Germany, immortalised in the poetry of Robert Browning; but there is a basic difference. Hamlyn's legend certainly recalls the past, but that legend influences its people's lives only insofar as the memory of the Pied Piper is recalled and represented for tourists; whereas Walsingham's past lives now as a present reality. Here, Mary seems present just as much as when Richeldis established her little chapel in honour of the Annunciation and the men and women of medieval England, as well as pilgrims from abroad, thronged to the village that held a shrine ranking in importance with Jerusalem, Rome and Compostella. Pilgrims come here today too in their thousands, but Walsingham retains its pristine simplicity, remembering always its *raison d'etre* to pay homage to Mary's joy and humility at the moment of the Annunciation.

PLAN of the medieval Augustinian Priory (now known locally as 'the Abbey'). All that is left of the great Church is the arch of the East window. The site of the original holy house is marked by a small stone slab set in the ground.

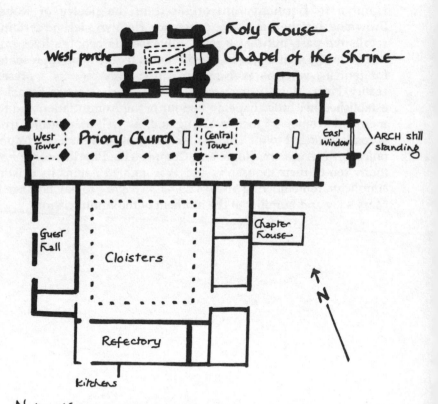

West porch

Holy House
Chapel of the Shrine

West Tower

Priory Church

Central Tower

East Window

ARCH still standing

Guest Hall

Cloisters

Chapter House

N

Refectory

Kitchens

Note: thick walls of shrine chapel
      alignment not quite parallel with church
          indicating separate construction
              prior to larger building

Walsingham – in you is built New Nazareth,
where shall be held in constant memory
the great joy of my salutation,
first of my joys – their foundation and origin,
root of humankind's gracious redemption.
When Gabriel gave me this news:
to be a mother through humility
and God's Son conceive in virginity.

(Pynson Ballad)

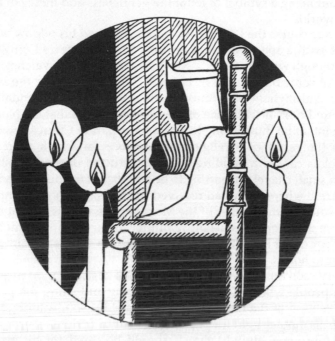

1. *The Story of a Shrine*

SOMETIME after the survey of England contained in Domesday book (completed 1084) a Norman knight, one who had possibly accompanied William the Conqueror on his expedition to England, was given the manor of Walsingham Parva, Little Walsingham, in Norfolk. It was a good place to live, fine farmlands, sheep, a river. He married a Saxon woman and settled down to bring up his family far from the familiar landscape of his native Normandy. His wife Richeldis was a woman well fitted to be lady of the manor. She knew the surrounding people and countryside, their history and religious background. Besides which she was known for her virtuous life and practical piety. It was the era of the Crusades. Jerusalem had been taken by the Christian forces under Godfrey de Bouillon in 1099 and there was a renewed interest in the Holy Land and the Christ who had lived and loved in historical Palestine. It was a time too of Marian piety, the Mother of the

Saviour being a symbol of feminine gentleness and mercy in a war-torn world.

In due course the Lord of the manor died and his widow was left alone with a son Geoffrey. Geoffrey, born and reared on English soil, though with his father's Norman surname de Favarches, was a man of some importance in Norfolk. Beside inheriting the land of Little Walsingham he witnessed the signing of the foundation of Binham Priory in 1108, one of the Cluniac houses that the Normans were intent on introducing to England as part of Church reform.

As the result of a religious experience (of which more later) Richeldis caused a building to be constructed of wooden slabs. It was a small chapel purporting to be a replica of the original house at Nazareth where Mary had received the message from an angel that she would be the mother of the Messiah. The widow used it for her private devotions, a constant reminder to her of another mother in the hour of her joy, a way of bringing the newly opened Holy Land closer to home.

Very soon this chapel became a place of special importance to the local people who recognised in its raising and siting the personal intervention of the mother of God. Richeldis' son, wanting to preserve his mother's gift for posterity, arranged (prior to journeying to the Holy Land himself) that it should be cared for by his clerk, Edwy, and ultimately become the property of a religious Order. To this end he settled on it the revenues of parts of his demense and the tithes, rents and dues of the parish Church. This document, undated but presumably from the first half of the twelfth century, is the first mention of a special chapel that we have. We know that a Geoffrey de Favarches had died before 1130 as there is another document in which William de Hocton 'answers for 30s for the manor of Wighton (close to Walsingham) and ten marks to marry Geoffrey's widow and bring up her son until he attains his majority'. However, in neither document is the woman named. Was the Richeldis of the Walsingham legend the *mother* of the first Geoffrey (signatory of the Binham Charter) or was she his *widow* (whose son presumably bore the same name and who, when he came of age went to Jerusalem, leaving the chapel in the care of Edwy his clerk some twenty years later)? This we shall never know unless further documentation should come to light, but my own preference is towards the conclusion that Richeldis was the first Geoffrey's mother rather than his wife, for if she had remarried so soon would posterity have remembered her as a widow? I doubt it.

The above reconstruction is my tentative re-telling of the origins of the shrine at Walsingham. The only extant narrative version of events is contained in the Pynson Ballad, so called because it was printed by Richard Pynson in 1493, though most likely it dates from around 1465. This Ballad gives the foundation date of the shrine as 1061, during the reign of St Edward the Confessor. However, there is always a tendency to push dates back to prove antiquity and there are other reasons, to which I will allude later, which might account for placing the shrine's foundation during the reign of the Confessor. Serious historians do not countenance this as factual; all look to a beginning in the first half of the twelfth century. The Pynson Ballad, written towards the end of the fifteenth century, cannot be relied on in this matter, especially as there is no record of a de Favarches family in the Domesday Book. That does not mean that the underlying truth of the ballad and all that the story symbolises has nothing to say to the men and women of our own day – far from it. But as far as possible we want to reach the facts behind the legend. The story of Walsingham is rich enough as it is, it is not necessary to insist on a pre-conquest foundation date that seems to have no real historical basis.

Returning to known historical facts, by 1153 a priory had been established according to the expressed wishes of Geoffrey de Favarches and the little chapel placed in the care of Augustinian canons. An Augustinian house did not need the kind of financial outlay required by a big monastery and would be within the capacity of a lord of a small manor who could not possibly endow a large Benedictine or Cistercian foundation. In 1159 Geoffrey's charter was confirmed by the Bishop of Norwich, the patrons being Robert de Brucurt (De Burgh) and Roger Earl of Clare, both of powerful and influential families whose descendants would later be involved in priory affairs. Of the de Favarches we hear no more. Either the male line died out or the family name was changed to Walsingham. The Augustinian canons enclosed Richeldis' 'Nazareth house' in their Lady Chapel, and later a statue was added depicting Mary with the child on her lap. The statue is of later twelfth or early thirteenth century provenance and is similar in some respects to the statues of Our Lady of Rocamodour and Our Lady of Montserrat, both of which were carved about the same time.

*Present Statue of
Our Lady of
Walsingham,
Slipper Chapel.*

As a place of pilgrimage, Walsingham seems to have grown very slowly. For more than a century the priory remained a place of only medium importance and wealth, the shrine of Little St William at Norwich eclipsing it both in fame and as a centre of healing and miracles. Walsingham's popularity suddenly rose to ascendancy during the reign of Henry III, son of King John of Magna Carta fame and nephew of the crusader King Richard, Coeur de Lion. Henry succeeded to the throne at the age of nine in 1217, and his majority was declared when he was nineteen by his principal tutor Hurbert de Burgh. Like Edward the Confessor, whom he chose as his model and patron, Henry was personally loveable but not a particularly strong or wise ruler. As a patron of arts and culture he set about cathedral building, especially enriching Westminster Abbey with precious relics and arranging for the tombs of the Plantagenets to cluster around that of the Confessor. He married Eleanor of Provence by whom he had two sons and three daughters. Theirs was an idyllic home life which deeply affected their son and heir, who wept so much on hearing of the death of his father that his courtiers reproached him, pointing out that he had not wept so at the death of his own child. 'I may have other children' replied the grieving man, 'but only one father, and what a father!'

Henry was genuinely religious, but his interest in Walsingham might never have been kindled except for the fact that in 1220 the priory of Bromholm (twenty five miles from Walsingham and near the Norfolk coast) acquired via the Crusades a relic reputed to be of the Holy Cross. The cleric who had it in his possession had already given two fingers of St Margaret and some jewelled crosses to St Alban's abbey, but no one seemed interested in the plain splinters of wood arranged in crosswise fashion. So, on entering Bromholm priory, (up until then an obscure house dependent on much larger Castle Acre) he took the relic with him as well as his two children.

Immediately the Holy Rood of Bromholm became a focal point for extraordinary miracles and in 1226 Henry, then aged eighteen, went to see it. While at Bromholm he granted the brothers a fair on the vigil, day and morrow of the feast of the Holy Cross. En route to the priory the king happened to stay two days at Walsingham where he also visited the holy house and granted the canons the right to a weekly market and a fair on the vigil and day of the Holy Cross. This points to Walsingham as being currently second in importance to Bromholm, for it was granted a smaller fair and that on Bromholm's patronal feast.

But this state of affairs speedily changed. Henry was at Walsingham again in 1229, 1232, 1235, 1242. He provided a consignment of oak trees for building, paid for 3,000 tapers to burn in the holy house on the feast of the Assumption, gave gold for a crown for Our Lady's statue, an embroidered chasuble and other rich gifts. In 1251 he gave leave for a fair to be held on the vigil and feast of Mary's nativity and for six days afterwards.

Henry's deep devotion to the shrine was passed on to his son Edward I, named for the Confessor, and one of England's greatest kings. He has been likened to king Alfred, a monarch both truly royal and yet at home with all classes of people.

Henry III is said to have been the first genuinely English king after the Conquest and the first to promulgate an official document

in the English language. Edward I continued in like manner and by
the time of his death had made England one of the leading nation
states, endeavouring to unite Scotland and Wales to his patrimony.
On a personal level he felt he owed his life to Our Lady of Walsingham when the roof under which he had been sitting just a moment
before caved in during a game of chess. Edward had been on cru-
sade to the Holy Land (and was actually abroad when news of his
father's death reached him). He had loved and admired Henry,
appreciated his home life and so kept up the pilgrimage tradition –
to England's Nazareth.

Edward is recorded as being in Walsingham on twelve occasions,
only two in Bromholm. In 1296 he or his envoys signed a treaty with
the count of Flanders in the Holy House itself, showing what importance he attached to the shrine. His son Edward II, while keeping up
the tradition of pilgrimage, was a weak and ineffectual ruler, an out-
door type of man, simple and straight-forward. Deposed by his wife
Isabella and her lover Mortimer he was forced to abdicate in favour
of his son, another Edward. The story ended with Edward II being
murdered in an indescribably horrible manner. Edward III thus
owed his throne to the adultery of his mother and the treachery of
Mortimer. Mortimer was duly executed and Isabella sent into permanent retirement at Castle Rising in Norfolk; therefore her son was
able to combine visits to his mother (who lived another thirty years)
with pilgrimages to the shrine in the same county. Edward was
married to Phillippa of Hainault, a gentle and merciful woman with
whom he lived very happily. Under his and Phillippa's patronage
the Lady of Clare (also founder of Clare College, Cambridge)
brought the Franciscans to Walsingham, much to the distress of the
Augustinians who feared they would appropriate alms destined for
the shrine. The Inn, the Black Lion, is said to be named for Edward's
queen, as the lion was the heraldic beast of the house of Hainault.
Edward III, like his grandfather, was an enormously popular ruler
and enjoyed a long reign.

An indication of the growing national and international importance of the shrine during the 'century of the Edwards' is the record
of countless royal and noble men and women travelling Walsing-
ham-wards both from England and abroad. Besides the aristocracy
there were numerous ordinary pilgrims, including many sick, all
hoping for a cure at Our Lady's intercession. Those coming by sea
disembarked at Lynn, those journeying overland made their way

from all corners of England, so much so that the Milky Way was renamed the Walsingham Way pointing, as it was said, the path to the virgin's own house.

In 1338 the Slipper Chapel at Houghton St Giles was built. Dedicated to St Catherine of Alexandria, the patron saint of pilgrims, it was so constructed that the sun rose directly behind the altar on her feast day, November 25th. In this little chapel pilgrims would remove their shoes and walk barefoot the last Holy Mile before entering the priory grounds at the end of their journey.

Something of the deep influence of Walsingham as the place where there was recalled perpetually the mystery of the Annunciation can be gleaned from the English devotion to Our Lady's joys and Julian of Norwich's own vision of our Lady at that most important moment when the Word was made flesh in her womb:

> Then he brought our Lady St Mary to my attention. I saw her spiritually in bodily likeness, a simple humble maiden, young in years and little more than a child, in the form in which she was when she conceived. God also showed me something of the wisdom and truth of her soul, and through this I understood her sense of reverence with which she beheld God, her creator. I also understood her profound wondering reverence that he, her creator, should want to be born of her, someone so simple and of his own making. This wisdom and truth, this knowledge of her creator's greatness and her own littleness as creature, made her say to Gabriel in deep humility: 'Behold me here, God's handmaiden!' In this vision I understood without any doubt that, as far as worthiness and wholeness are concerned, she is superior to everything else that God has made; for above her there is nothing in the created order except Jesus Christ in his humanity, as I see it.[1]

Can it then be wondered at that by the time the Pynson Ballad was written, when Walsingham had been for some time a shrine of equal importance to the other major shrines of Christendom – Rome, Jerusalem and Compostella – England had become known as Our Lady's Dowry, renowned for its devotion to the Mother of God, and Walsingham a holy land likened to Nazareth itself. The house, enhoused in the priory church, was a place sacred to numerous medieval men and women who converged on the spot eager for

water from the holy wells, looking for cures, agog to see the miraculous statue and to pray within the walls of Richeldis' chapel, recall-
ing the joy of the Annunciation.

But it can surely be seen too how by this time the shrine's
foundation was being traced to the reign of Edward the Confessor.
Three Edwards, all named for this saint, had made Walsingham
their royal choice. The shrine was intimately connected with kings
who had made England great. And who was Richeldis? Her history
was shrouded in antiquity. To place her therefore in the era of the
Confessor was to give Walsingham an added drawing power and it
was only a matter of a few decades to push back the founding date.
This is not to say that the records we have were planned deliber-
ately to confuse or deceive. The shrine had begun in relative obscu-
rity; it must have been many years before it became necessary to
search out the truth of its origins. And basically I feel sure that
the story contained in the Pynson Ballad is true in its broadest out-
lines. But to say that the shrine began in Saxon times does not seem
consonant with the documentary evidence available, meagre
though it is.

Royal pilgrims continued to come to Walsingham right up to the
time of the English Reformation. Henry VIII and Katherine of
Aragon his queen both came on different occasions. Henry VIII
manifested a special devotion to the shrine, having a candle burning
there perpetually for his intentions. He is said to have walked the
holy mile from Barsham Manor, a great house near the Slipper
Chapel, which is still standing today. It was to Walsingham that
Henry rode post haste through the snow and slush to give thanks
for the birth of a son, born to him in January 1511 but who died in
February of the same year. How different history might have been
had the infant Henry survived! How different the fate of poor
Katherine who died unloved and rejected, leaving instructions that
a pilgrim should go to Walsingham on her behalf after her death to
pray for her soul and distribute alms en route.

It is a moving imaginary exercise to see with the mind's eye the
shrine as it was in medieval times: the rich offerings left before Our
Lady, the crush of Christians high and low venerating the statue,
the canons ever present to collect gifts in the holy house, the sick
bathing in the wells, the shouting innkeepers, the beggars, the lepers ... But none of these are the reason for Walsingham's fame; that
was, and always will be, the commemoration of Mary's salutation in

a simple ordinary home. There seems to be no special 'message' attached to Walsingham, nothing in the way of requests to live lives of prayer or penance or fasting. There is just a desire for others to find joy in Our Lady's joy with no self regard whatsoever. Surely that is better than anything else that could be devised: the 'Ave' bell ringing over the village and the pilgrims rejoicing in Mary's joy.

Walsingham remained a focus for English Marian devotion until the dissolution of the monasteries. However, the affairs of the priory had seldom been of the most edifying. Various irregularities among the canons, disputes, interdicts, rumours of mismanagement of property seem to have surfaced at regular intervals. It is not for nothing that the gospel warns against the corrupting power of riches, and by this time Walsingham was the richest religious house in England. When the King's ministers arrived the canons handed over the country's most sacred shrine without a murmur, the prior, Richard Vowell, being the first of the community to sign the oath of supremacy which recognised Henry as head of the Church in England. The rest of the canons followed suit, with the dubious honour of being the first major religious house to capitulate.

Nevertheless the priory continued to open its doors to pilgrims, though the end could only now be a matter of time. When Norfolk people expressed their displeasure at the suppression of the smaller monastic houses in the area (of which there were many) the ringleaders were denounced and put to death, one of them being the Walsingham sub-prior, Nicholas Mileham. The suspicion for Nicholas' betrayal points to his own prior which makes the whole business doubly distasteful.

In 1538 the image of our Lady was removed from her chapel and all precious objects confiscated. The original image disappeared without trace, burnt at Smithfield, though there is a hope in some hearts that the statue was secretly taken abroad and a substitute consigned to the flames. This has actually proved to be the case with Our Lady of Ipswich, the original being smuggled out of the country to become 'The English Madonna' at Nettuno in Italy.

The holy house was burned to the ground. For a short while the canons continued in possession until they too were finally dispersed on October 20th 1539. The Franciscan friary met the same fate, passing into the hands of the king's sympathisers. The sacred buildings, left untenanted and uncared for fell into ruin. Walsingham sank back into being an ordinary Norfolk village although memories of its former glory never completely disappeared.

In 1578 Queen Elizabeth I made a royal progress through the county. On this occasion it is possible that the Walsingham Lament was composed by someone in her entourage such as Philip Howard, Earl of Arundel, who would later be imprisoned in the tower and become a martyr for the Catholic faith.

ELIZABETHAN LAMENT FOR WALSINGHAM

In the wreck of Walsingham
Whom should I choose
But the Queen of Walsingham
To be guide to my muse?

Then, thou Prince of Walsingham,
Grant me to frame
Bitter 'plaints to rue thy wrong,
Bitter woe for thy name.

Bitter was it oh to see
The silly sheep,
Murdered by the ravening wolves
While the shepherds did sleep.

Bitter was it oh to view
The sacred vine
(While the gardeners played so close)
Rooted up by the swine.

Bitter, bitter to behold
The grass to grow,
Where the walls of Walsingham
So stately did show.

Such was the worth of Walsingham
While she did stand,
Such are the ruins as now do show
Of that most holy land.

Level, level with the ground
The towers do lie,
Which with their golden glittering tops
Pierced up to the sky.

Where were gates no gates are now,
The ways unknown
Where the press of friars did pass,
While her fame far was blown.

Owls do screech where sweetest hymns
Lately were sung,
Toads and serpents hold their dens
Where the pilgrims did throng.

Weep weep O Walsingham,
Whose days are nights,
Blessings turned to blasphemies,
Holy deeds to despites.

Sin is where Our Lady sat,
Heaven turned to hell;
Satan sits where our Lord held sway,
Walsingham oh farewell!

(Anon – slightly modernised)

So passed England's glory, awaiting a new birth, a new life when the time was right.

NOTE

1 Julian of Norwich. *Revelations of Divine Love* Ch. 4. Unpublished translation by J. Pischler.

2. *Richeldis and her Chapel*

What can we glean of Walsingham's origins and message from the only account we have of the Shrine's beginnings? The Pynson Ballad, although written only a few decades before the shrine's dissolution, obviously purports to tell a story that reaches far back into the past. It is a truism that 'nothing comes from nothing'. Someone, at some time, had erected the holy house that stood in the Lady Chapel of the great priory church – but who? how? why? and when?

This is the story as we now have it, modernised and slightly adapted.

THE PYNSON BALLAD

This chapel was founded in the year of the Incarnation 1061, during the reign of St Edward, King of this land.

All you spiritual people who are devoted to this place, asking our Lady for succour, wanting her help in tribulation, you can learn how this chapel was founded if you just read this tablet, it tells the story of a miracle.

A noble widow, Richeldis, at one time a lady of the manor and known for her virtuous life, asked our Lady if she could honour her in a special way. This blessed and gracious virgin granted her request in the manner I shall describe, asking her to build this chapel.

In spirit our Lady led Richeldis to Nazareth and showed her the house where the angel Gabriel had greeted her. 'Look daughter', said our Lady 'Take the measurements of this place and make another like it at Walsingham for my praise and special honour. Everyone who comes to me there shall find help.

'It shall be a perpetual memorial to the great joy of my Salutation, the first of my joys, their ground and origin, root of humankind's gracious redemption. This happened when Gabriel gave me the message that I was to be a mother owing to my humility, and conceive God's son in virginity.'

The devout woman was shown this vision three times and mentally she noted exactly the length and breadth of the building. Full of gladness she thanked our Lady who never deserts the needy. That very same hour, not wishing to waste a minute, she summoned the best architects to design the chapel according to our Lady's instructions.

That night a meadow was soaked with heavenly dew sent down by Mary, except for two places which remained dry. This was the first intimation of where our new Nazareth should stand, built like the first one in the Holy Land.

When everything was ready, Richeldis was in a quandary. In which of the two places marked by the miraculous intervention of our Lady should the house be set? Two equal areas had been left dry in the midst of the dew (like Gideon's fleece).

The widow thought the best site to build on was the site where the chapel of St Lawrence now stands, close by the two wells. (Visitors to the place are familiar with it).

The carpenters set to work to raise the holy house, but they were soon baffled by the fact that nothing seemed to fit together properly despite their best efforts. They felt very discouraged at their failure.

At last they laid their tools aside and Richeldis bade them go off and rest. Meanwhile she prayed devoutly to our Lady to bring the work to a proper conclusion and guide her as to what to do next.

The widow remained in prayer all night. Meanwhile, by the hands of angels, our Lady not only raised the house (she being its chief architect) but also set it two hundred feet or more away from the first site. Books mention this.

When the builders came back early to continue their work they found every part faultlessly joined, far better than they could have done it themselves. So each man returned to his home, and the holy matron thanked our Lady for the great favour she had shown.

Since then our Lady has performed many miracles here, too many to tell. For more than four hundred years the chronicles bear witness that those who visit her dwelling by coming here on pilgrimage, or calling on her in distress, have received grace down through the ages.

Many sick have been cured by our Lady's power, the dead revived, the lame made whole, the blind have had their sight restored. Mariners have been brought safely to port through tempest and storm. Deaf-mutes, lunatics and lepers have all been made well through our Lady's intercession.

People troubled by evil spirits have been delivered from them. Also souls suffering from spiritual temptation have found comfort. Every tribulation, bodily or spiritual, can find a remedy here by devoutly calling on our Lady.

Therefore, pilgrims all, strive to serve our Lady here with humble affection. Apply yourself to doing as she would wish, remembering the great joy of her Annunciation. This brief ballad, though lacking in metre and eloquence, is written in her honour.

Educated folk with more intelligence can learn more about the founding of this chapel by consulting books. The chronicles can help you understand the whole history and circumstances of this place, for they bear witness to it.

O England you have every reason to be happily compared to the promised land of Sion. This glorious lady's grace and support enable you to be called everywhere the holy land, our Lady's Dowry, as you have been named from the beginning.

The likely cause of this title is that here is built this house in new Nazareth, to the honour of the Queen of Heaven and her glorious Salutation. 'Ave', Gabriel's greeting in old Nazareth, is daily remembered here as your joy.

O gracious lady, glory of Jerusalem, cypress of Sion, joy of Israel, rose of Jericho, star of Bethlehem, do not despise our petitions. You are the most merciful of women, therefore grant your bounteous grace to all who devoutly visit you here.

The first thing to strike the careful reader is the person of Richeldis. She is a wellborn woman, a widow of means, who asks our Lady for a way to honour her. Richeldis is not a 'visionary' as, for example, are Bernadette of Lourdes, Mariette Beco of Banneux or the children of Fatima. None of these were asking for or expecting anything particular when they 'saw' our Lady, and all of them were children. Richeldis on the other hand is a mature woman who wants to use her wealth wisely in honouring our Lady and so she prays for a way to do so. She ponders, meditates, prays.

Our Lady then leads Richeldis 'in spirit' to Nazareth and shows her the house where the angel greeted her at the Annunciation. As far as I can see this is not necessarily a 'vision' of Mary. Richeldis may well have heard returning crusaders tell of Nazareth, and in her meditation 'seen' the place in her mind's eye. One aspect of the story which seems to validate this interpretation is that nowhere is a 'vision' of our Lady referred to as the miracle of Walsingham. The 'miracle' lies in the siting and raising of the house in the place where our Lady wished it to stand. Any vision is obviously of the house *in situ* at Nazareth, not of Mary herself.

The mystery of the Incarnation, origin and ground of Mary's joy, is to be commemorated anew at Walsingham by Richeldis erecting a house of similar proportions to the one at Nazareth.

As soon as Richeldis is sure that this is what Mary wants of her,

'not wishing to waste a minute', (an echo of the Visitation where
Mary goes 'in haste' to Elizabeth to share and communicate her joy
in the 'Magnificat') she immediately sets to work, employing architects and builders to realise her plans.

This is a further indication that no external appearance of our
Lady was involved. In these cases there is nearly always some
necessity for ecclesiastical approval and inquiry. But Richeldis acts
alone. She has money. She consults with no bishop or priest. She is
an independent women acting on what she considers a personal
inspiration, the fruit of prayer.

But where should the holy house be erected? It is here that the
chronicler points to miraculous intervention by referring to a
biblical episode, that of Gideon's fleece in the book of Judges.
(cf Ju 6.36–40) Gideon, wanting a sign from God that he has truly
been chose to deliver Israel from its enemies, lays a fleece on his
threshing floor, saying that if God sends dew on the fleece but
leaves the ground dry he will accept this as a sign from heaven.
God obliges, but Gideon is still not satisfied and asks for the
miracle to be reversed – the fleece left dry and the ground dew-
soaked.

In Medieval times the presence of our Lady was often thought to
be signified by dew or rain and biblical texts were interpreted
accordingly. Elijah's vision of a little cloud rising out of the sea and
presaging an end of Israel's drought was given a Marian interpretation. The site of the basilica of St Mary Major in Rome, the oldest
church in Europe dedicated to the Mother of God, was said to have
been marked by a miraculous fall of snow (leading to the title of Our
Lady of the Snows). A Vespers antiphon for January 1st, feast of the
Mother of God, contains the following words 'Your mysterious
birth from the holy virgin fulfills the ancient sign. Rain comes down
to soak the fleece, token of your saving presence, O Lord our God
we cry out in wonder'. Another Advent antiphon speaks of the Lord
coming down gently, like rain on the grass, into the womb of the
Virgin. All these images refer to the hidden and mysterious way
that Jesus, Son of God and son of Mary took flesh in the womb of his
mother – the mystery that was to be, and still is, at the heart of
Walsingham.

However, the way ahead for Richeldis in choosing a site is confused by the fact that two areas are indicated as possible choices.
Which one shall she choose? According to legend the first choice by

the two wells proved impossible, as the builders could not make the prepared wooden slabs fit properly.

Richeldis then sought further guidance by a night vigil of prayer, during which time the chapel was raised by angels on the second site, where it continued to stand for posterity. Maybe here is a confused memory of the chapel having once been at another location. Could it have been built first by the wells and later dismantled and re-erected in the Lady chapel of the Priory? It seems unlikely.

Whatever may be the case, it is certain that the wooden house itself was an object of great veneration. In general the people of medieval times had little respect for ancient buildings and, where possible, rebuilt them on a larger and more ornate scale. A priory as wealthy as Walsingham became in the course of years could easily have afforded a more sumptuous memorial to our Lady's Annunciation. The facts that the original wooden chapel was left untouched is a sure sign that it was considered to be of exceptional significance.

Another shrine of the holy house, this time at Loreto in Italy, also has a history of being moved. It purports to be the *actual* house of the Annunciation, transported by the hands of angels from Nazareth to Tersatto in Yugoslavia in 1291, then to Recanti in Italy in 1294 and twice again in 1295 when it reached its present resting place at Loreto where it reposes in a great basilica. As these dates are well after Walsingham's foundation, and the Loreto house claims to be the *actual* house of Nazareth (which Walsingham has never purported to be) it is difficult to know whether the Loreto story later influenced the Pynson Ballad or not.

Once the chapel at Walsingham had been erected, the story goes that it speedily became a place of pilgrimage where numerous miracles were worked, though historical evidence points to a more gradual development. It is unfortunate that the books and chronicles referred to in the ballad have disappeared completely.

We may know of royal pilgrims but what of the numerous ordinary people who made their way to Walsingham to pray or to seek a cure? One hint we have is found in the Paston Letters when in 1443 Margaret Paston writes to her husband:

> My mother promised another image of wax of the weight of you to our Lady of Walsingham and she sent four nobles to the four Orders of Friars in Norwich [*viz.* Franciscans, Dominicans,

Carmelites and Augustinians] to pray for you, and I have promised to go on pilgrimage to Walsingham and St Leonard's for you.

The custom of donating life size wax figures to shrines still pertains in Portugal where similar effigies can be seen at Fatima. No wonder that the chapel was always brightly lit, ablaze with splendour. It makes one wonder whether in fact the image of our Lady that was venerated there was actually dark. Close examination of the 'dark Virgin' of Montserrat has led to the conclusion that the dark faces of mother and child are due to being long exposed in a small chapel to numerous candles, whose smoke has gradually impregnated the wood and turned it black.

Walsingham is a place to remember Mary's joy. The pilgrims are not there only to seek miracles and cures. They are to do as Mary would wish and as she has done herself – open themselves to the fulfilling of God's will in their own lives.

The themes of the Pynson Ballad as we have it today can be summed up in the following words:

Joy and gladness – for Mary and for all humanity
humility
prayer
God's love for the sick and needy (the 'anawim',
the little ones of this world)
Our Lady and the Incarnation (God-with-us)

The ballad ends with an explanation of why England has been given the ancient title of Our Lady's Dowry. It is because Nazareth has been realised again in Walsingham, making of England another Holy Land.

The final verse, a prayer to our Lady, combines two biblical texts, from the deuterocanonical books of Sirach and Judith:

So I was established in Sion
and in Jerusalem was my dominion.
I took root in an honoured people
in the portion of the Lord who is their inheritance.
I grew tall like a cypress on the heights of Hermon
and like a rose plant in Jericho.   (Sir 24.10–14)

and

> You are the exaltion of Jerusalem
> you are the great glory of Israel,
> you are the great pride of our nation.   (Jud 15.9)

Judith was a brave widow who courageously trusted the Lord against all odds, praying in the following words:

> For your power depends not upon numbers
> nor your might upon men of strength.
> For you are a God of the lowly,
> helper of the oppressed,
> upholder of the weak,
> Saviour of those without hope.   (Jud 9.11)

Richeldis, like Judith, and indeed like Mary herself, was used by God to forward his designs – not by force or power but by openness and a spirit of trust; for he is 'a God of the lowly.'

Richeldis is therefore presented to us as one of the biblical 'anawim' those poor and humble Israelites who inherit the promises and depend wholly on God, not their own merits and virtue.

> I will leave in the midst of you a people humble and lowly.
> They shall seek refuge in the name of the Lord
> those who are left in Israel.   (Zeph 3.12)

The first chapters of Luke's gospel portray the faithful remnant in whom God is able to fulfil his designs. There we meet Zechariah and Elizabeth, elderly and barren, Mary the virgin from gentile Galilee, Simeon and Anna, old yet still patiently waiting for salvation.

In the Old Testament widows, orphans and strangers (foreigners) have rights peculiar to themselves. They have a right to glean (as Ruth gleans in the fields of Boaz) a right to be protected and treated with justice and charity. Ruth, both foreigner and widow is chosen as a foremother of the Davidic Messianic line, notwithstanding all human considerations to the contrary.

Opposite: A pilgrimage entering the Priory Grounds (Photo: Louis Quail).

God often chooses the spiritually poor for a special mission, simply because in them power is seen to be made perfect in weakness: Gideon, Deborah, Judith, Esther, Jeremiah ... Even Israel herself is chosen for love alone, not because she has 'earned' the Lord's favour:

> You are a people holy to the Lord your God ... It is not because you were great that the Lord chose you but simply because he loved you.   (cf Deut 7.7)

Throughout Christian history Marian shrines have been the result of God's same choice of the 'poor', of the unlikely candidate; Bernadette the asthmatic illiterate, the shepherds of Fatima, Mariette Beco, daughters of an unemployed labourer and known for her own sharp tongue. And those who respond are also mainly the poor – who reach out to symbols of hope: hope that God is concerned for them *now*, concerned for the needy, the sick, the oppressed, those who do not count in the corridors of power.

At Walsingham, Richeldis too, despite her seeming wealth and social position comes into the biblical category of 'little ones'. She is a widow. She is the wife of a foreigner and possibly foreign born herself. She is anonymous like so many wives and mothers, her son does not even mention her name in deeding her chapel to become a religious foundation.

Like the widow of Luke's gospel who gave her mite, 'all that she had', so Richeldis gave 'all that she had' to honour another woman: a woman who had been a joyful girl at the Annunciation, but also a wife and widow, the mother of a son as Richeldis herself had been.

True poverty and dependence show a willingness to give God whatever he asks, great or small, and to do so quietly and without blare of trumpets. In a way, poverty equals 'open-ness', readiness to change, to respond to grace offered, to be prepared to receive all from God, ready to reverse personal plans, as was Esther at Mordecai's bidding, or as Elijah on Horeb when the still small voice summoned him to action, or as Mary at the Annunciation.

Richeldis had asked for a way to honour our Lady, but she was open as regards the means. For this she sought God's will in prayer

Opposite (top) Entrance to Anglican Shrine; (below) Looking through into interior of the holy house, Anglican Shrine (photos: Louis Quail).

and meditation. Hers is not a 'magic' story, but one of human search and co-operation with grace. She is so transparent she literally fades into the background once her task is accomplished – as Mary disappears from the picture during Jesus' public life. Richeldis is a woman who knew all the seasons of a woman's life-experience: girlhood and virginity, wifehood, human fruitfulness in physical maternity, deprivation and barrenness in the widowed state. She does not even have the 'richness' of being proclaimed a saint. There appears to have been no spontaneous veneration of her person as one who had 'seen' our Lady, no cult of her sanctity, no tradition that she later entered religious life or took up residence near her chapel as an anchoress. Indeed it is possible that she remarried. We do not know.

Richeldis is born, grows, marries, becomes a mother, then a widow. She is used by God for a certain work. She dies. Maybe she was not even particularly holy. Nevertheless, she stands as a symbol of countless women who have 'done what they could' for God and been content. Therefore the place in which she honoured the mother of God has become a holy place, a new Nazareth for countless generations.

3. Symbol of the House

RICHELDIS had arranged for a house to be built at Walsingham on the pattern of Mary's house at Nazareth – a perpetual reminder of the joy she experienced at the Annunciation.

Here then are two themes held in tension – the theme of stability and security symbolised by the house, and the theme of open-ness to the Spirit: a readiness for change, for the unexpected, for the welcome of new life as depicted in the story of the Annunciation.

As a focus of devotion, the holy house was a small wooden building 23½ ft x 12 ft 10 in, possibly approximating what a poor Norfolk family might consider adequate for basic shelter, but certainly bearing no resemblance to the fine flint castles and manor houses that were the domains of the rich.

This little wooden edifice was preserved within the Lady Chapel of the priory which built a great church to 'house the house'. And inside the house was the venerated statue of mother and child, stately, serene, welcoming. So, the mother seated in the house emphasises stability, while the commemoration of the Annunciation emphasises open-ness, fluidity, responsiveness to the unpredictable and unsettling.

However, without the first quality of stability there is no chance of the second blossoming. Without basic security one lives in too much fear to face an unpredictable future with confidence.

In medieval Norfolk, Mary's house at Walsingham must have had added significance. Norfolk, even in Saxon times, was a relatively wealthy county due to the sheep which pastured in large flocks on the marshes. But there were also many peasants trying to eke a living out of the soil where crops were grown in rotation and the manor system of strip farming prevailed. These men and women, born to labour and hardship, knowing only the Church's holy days as holidays, must often have felt alienated from their overlords in castles and monasteries. Norfolk, with its flat landscape and great arching sky, was exposed to the biting ocean winds which swept over field and fen, chilling the poorly clad. Its isolated labourers were far from the cultural and religious centres of influence and thus ripe for Richeldis' initiative. To the peasants, home was everything. Across the flat fields, the sight of one's little house standing firm signified that one 'belonged' somewhere; that in the large, frightening, often threatening world, there was a centre that held firm.

These were times too of social upheaval. The Conquest and its aftermath, civil war during the reign of Stephen and Matilda, warring barons, the call to the crusades and local feuds all took their toll of human life. Fatal diseases spread quickly when people were without access to proper medical care. Women frequently died in childbirth and infant mortality was high. All these factors combined to keep people aware of human vulnerability in the face of sickness and other elemental forces beyond their control.

While large and beautiful churches (and Norfolk excelled in building these as the wool trade developed) would lift the mind and heart heavenwards with the promise of a glorious paradise after death, Richeldis' small chapel, constructed to the proportions of the wattle and daub dwellings of the poor, would be a strong visual aid balancing the thought of heavenly glory with the realities of earthly existence. The house was a permanent reminder that the Incarnation and human birth of the Son of God took place among working folk. It focused the attention on Nazareth and the human Christ, not the resurrected Lord reigning in splendour.

A small chapel with a seated mother and child within spoke of God's nearness, his concern with the lesser ones of this world. It symbolised the way life endures from generation to generation in humble guise and by way of the natural generative processes that bind families together in a shared environment and experience; for the house of the Annunciation was soon identified with the memory of the house where Jesus grew up as the reputed son of the village carpenter.

We are learning more and more that to be homeless is to feel oneself to be less of a person. One needs to belong somewhere, put down roots, build a human life from a base where one is respected and accepted for what one is. A house is far more than a building, it embodies all that people mean when they talk of 'home'.

At the heart of Christianity lies the mystery of the Incarnation, 'the Word was made flesh'. It was Mary's preparedness that enabled her to receive the seed of the Word that he might grow within her, become literally 'flesh of her flesh'. It was a seed rooted in the soil of her strong love, destined to blossom into the One who reigned from the great tree of the cross:

> None in foliage, none in blossom,
> none in fruit thy peer may be.
> Fairest wood and fairest iron
> Fairest weight is hung on thee.
>
> (Passiontide hymn)

At the beginning of his human life Jesus, like all infants, needed a place to come to; a place within his mother's womb and a place of nurture at Nazareth. He too needed house and home.

Jung says that the essence of a symbol is that it represents something not entirely understandable. A symbol operates at many levels of consciousness and has to be lived with in order to be penetrated. The house is one of these primary symbols – like bread, mother, water. In dreams and in writing it is acknowledged to be one of the most common symbols of the person. It is especially applicable to women, for women are physiologically fashioned with inner space to bear children, and after birth it is generally their task to provide a home where the child can develop into a person able, in due course, to live a socially adjusted yet independent life in the larger world. The home is the 'womb' from which one is born into society, just as one first comes from the womb into the world of living beings as part of a family.

It would be interesting to search out and list the number of Marian shrines which have as their focus a tiny chapel, either within a larger church or standing alone. These speak of intimacy, enveloping tenderness and the security of a mother's love. To name but a few: Portiuncula 'Our Lady of the Angels' at Assisi, and Loreto, both in Italy, Kleve in Germany, Sammarei in Bavaria, Banneux in France, and of course, Walsingham.

The house or tiny chapel not only commemorates the mystery of Mary's life and her continual presence among her children, it is a symbol of her person in virginity and in motherhood.

The book of Sirach depicts a woman in the following words:

> Like the sun rising in the heights of the Lord
> so is the beauty of a good wife in her
> well-ordered home.
> Like the shining lamp on the holy lampstand
> is a beautiful face on a stately figure.
> Like pillars of gold on a base of silver,
> so are beautiful feet with a steadfast
> heart.   (Sir 26.16–18)

Here we have an image of woman signified by the sun in its warmth, the light of a lamp as reflected in her radiant presence, and the pillars of practical devotion, imparting stability and strength.

The house image of Mary the virgin
In the wooden structure Richeldis erected at Walsingham there is symbolised Mary herself. The house commemorates not only the setting in which she uttered her 'yes' as she trustfully surrendered herself to the action of the Holy Spirit, but it is a 'picture' of who she was. It could be said that the house stands for Mary, empty and barren until made fruitful by the presence of the Word made flesh, just as the presence of a child transforms any home, making it radiant with the warmth of new life and love.

As we know, in the Old Testament virginity was not considered a

sign of God's choice and blessing but a sign of poverty and need.
The virgin is seen as barren, waiting for another to claim and fulfil
her. Her womb and her arms are empty until she is made fruitful in
marriage.

Israel, as bride of the Lord, *needs* her husband. In itself her virginity is not considered praiseworthy. It is so only insofar as it disposes
her to look to the Lord for fulfilment:

> You shall no more be termed forsaken
> and your land shall no more be termed desolate
[using the terms forsaken and desolate for virginity]
> But you shall be called 'my delight in her'
> and your land 'married'.
> For as a young man marries a virgin
> so shall the one who built you wed you
> And as the bridegroom rejoices over the bride
> so shall your God rejoice over you. (Is 62.4–5)

The Lord's dealings with his chosen people are designed to purify,
cleanse, 'virginise' them so that they know experientially their own
poverty, their inability to help themselves, and so cleave to him in
perfect trust.

> O afflicted one storm tossed and not comforted,
> behold I will lay your stones in antimony
> and lay your foundations with sapphires.
> I will make your pinnacles of agate, your
> gates of carbuncles and all your walls of
> precious stones.
> All your children shall be taught by the Lord
> and great shall be the prosperity of your
> children. (Is 54.11–13)

As the virgin leaves the home of her childhood to enter upon a new
life as wife and mother, so God prepares Israel to enter into a nup-
tial relationship with him. Virginity of itself means nothing. It is an
interim state, a preparation for something better and deeper.

The virgin Israel, the 'poor one' is, above all, personified in Mary,
daughter of Sion, loved and chosen to be God's home, his dwelling
place, her emptiness destined to be filled by him.

I have loved you with an everlasting love
therefore I have continued my faithfulness to you.
Again I shall build you and you shall be rebuilt
O virgin Israel.   (Jer. 31.3–4)

Mary is a virginal house, built by God for himself, ready to receive the Word made flesh. Her emptiness and expectancy are rooted deeply in her nation's religion and history. In her own body she bears the yearnings and hopes of generations of her people. She is the one who will open the Abrahamic and Davidic promises to the world. In her God will 'build a house' that endures forever. Caryll Houselander puts its poetically in this way:

> It was as if the human race were a little dark house, without light or air, locked and latched.
> The wind of the Spirit had beaten on the door, rattled the windows, tapped on the dark glass with tiny hands of flowers, flung golden seed against it, even, in hours of storm, lashed it with the boughs of a great tree, the prophecy of the cross – and yet the Spirit was outside. But one day a girl opened the door, and the little house was swept pure and sweet by the wind. Seas of light swept through it and the light remained in it; and in that little house a human child was born and the child was God. Our Lady said yes for the human race.[1]

Mary was enabled to say yes because within her she had empty space to fill. She was ready to welcome the Word because she had deep security in her identity. She personified a people led by the Lord at every point of their history. Our Lady, as Lightbearer, carries the light of the world in her own flesh which until then has been untilled and untenanted. But now the empty house is no longer empty: for see, she stands, the virgin, all light because she bears the Light.

The house as image of Mary the mother
If Mary the virgin is symbolised by light, joy and welcome 'the shining lamp on the holy lampstand'; then Mary the mother is symbolised by warmth 'the sun rising in the heights of the Lord'.

From the very beginning Walsingham was identified with the home of Nazareth, Mary being at its heart, just as the mother is, or should be, the heart of every home. If the empty house of the Annunciation is the image of Mary the Virgin, then the house of the family at Nazareth epitomises Mary as mother.

We can easily forget that Jesus *needed* Mary and Joseph to give him the security a child requires, offering him a place to grow from so that he could develop into the man he was destined to become – totally secure in the love of God his Father and thus able to go out to others in self-forgetfulness.

> God is love (wrote Dom Marmion) and that we may have some idea of that love he gives a share of it to mothers. The heart of a mother with her unwavering tenderness, the constancy of her solicitude, the inexhaustible delicacy of her affection is a truly divine creation, although God has placed in her only a spark of his love for us.[2]

At Nazareth Jesus received his first taste of love's sweetness within an ordinary Jewish home. So the holy house of Walsingham stands too for the sanctity of family life. Each home is to be a holy house where the Word becomes flesh once more among those who live there.

The gospels tell us little of the early life of Jesus, but we can surmise much from the picture they convey of his mother and foster father and from their portrayal of the adult man Jesus became. During his ministry he spoke with the confidence of a truly free person; he withdrew often for long, solitary nights of prayer; he was drawn upon incessantly by the multitude of sick and needy. Such a life could be borne only if his roots were deep. To be loved and to be secure in love is the only way people can live deeply. Because Jesus had been 'at home' in Nazareth he was able to live fully, trust the Father so confidently *anywhere*.

In seeing the house as an image of Mary the mother it reflects her stability, solidity, selfless love and practical devotion, taking place in the context of a Jewish home where the mother held an honoured place. A house which is a true home needs expanding walls to accommodate friends, relatives, travellers, and we must never forget the Jewish love of 'getting together' with the extended family. It is no coincidence I am sure that medieval Walsingham had a special place assigned to St Anne, mother of the mother of God.

Pondering on the symbolism of woman as house there came to

mind the figure of Ma Joad as she appears in Steinbeck's novel *The Grapes of Wrath*. This is how he describes Ma at the beginning of the book.

> Ma looked out into the sunshine. Her full face was not soft, it was controlled, kindly. Her hazel eyes seemed to have experienced all possible tragedy and to have mounted pain and suffering like steps into a calm and superhuman understanding. She seemed to know, to accept, to welcome her position, the citadel of the family, the strong place that could not be taken ... From her great and humble position in the family she had taken dignity and a clean, calm beauty. She seemed to know that if she swayed the family shook, and if ever she deeply despaired the family will to function would be gone.[3]

In the book, the story of the Joad family is told in the context of the history of Oklahoma, where the expanding dustbowl and the greed of owners are forcing smaller sharecroppers off the land. The Joads sell all and plan to move to California where they have heard that land, work and money are available. On the road they join the growing army of migrants living in vans and tents, desperate for employment. Uprooted from familiar surroundings they get poorer and more desperate even as they cherish the hope that California will prove a paradise at the end of the road. But once there they are employed in backbreaking toil – harvesting grapes, lettuces, cotton, peaches. Food is destroyed before their eyes to keep prices up while pickers starve.

The Joads experience appalling humiliations as they travel from farm to farm. It is a tale of exploitation, injustice, bullying, conditions of poverty and squalor below any standard befitting human dignity. The rich thrive while the poor slave in progressively worse surroundings – without food, education, medical care – treated worse than animals, as if without souls and without hope.

Yet at the centre of this degradation shines the figure of Ma – Ma Joad. A solid rock of support, a totally selfless woman who creates some kind of home out of each place the family goes to. She feeds and encourages husband and children, wears herself out for the family, always sees and believes the best; never gives up. Ma is no sylphlike, plaster Madonna figure, but a solid, mediterranean-type wife and mother; the image of stability in a world perpetually on the move. She is the centre, the lynch pin.

When the men cannot get work, when life bears down on them and poverty presses, when her pregnant daughter, Rose of Sharon's husband leaves her, Ma is there. It is Ma who helps Rose of Sharon move from the loneliness of a self-centred young girl to the fulness of a self-giving woman which climaxes the narrative.

Above all there is Ma's great love for her son Tom, who she knows is 'special' and who has far more within him than appears on the surface. When Tom in the struggle for justice gets into trouble with the police and has to go into hiding Ma knows there is no hope of a fair trial – how could there be? They are only 'Oakies'. Courageously she goes out to Tom one night and tells him that for his own safety he must leave the area. Although she has been stretched to the limit of her endurance and her little world is collapsing round her, Ma lets Tom go. She can only suffer inarticulately, for she has no words to express the love she feels for her boy and her helplessness before life's cruelty. Dumbly she hugs her son in the darkness, knowing he must go on with his mission, fulfil his own calling. Ma returns to her dwindling family, heart aching, yet smiling for the sake of others who are dependent on her and who will collapse if she collapses.

What an image Ma is of Mary in her fidelity to her Son from his birth to his passion! Mary too knew how to love in a way that, far from limiting her maternity, expanded it to admit John in the place of Jesus, and after him innumerable members of Christ – those who do his will and are therefore brother, sister, mother to him in their turn, those born of water and the Spirit through his painful sacrifice.

As with Ma Joad so with Mary. There is always room for one more, even in losing she gains. Life continues.

> 'Woman can change better'n a man' Ma said soothingly. 'Woman got all her life in her arms. Man got it all in his head ... We ain't gonna die out. People is goin' on – changing' a little maybe, but goin' right on'.[4]

In the book of Sirach we read of Wisdom personified: 'Like a vine I caused loveliness to bud and my blossoms bore glorious and abundant fruit'. (Sir. 24.17) These words are applied in the liturgy to Mary. They sound poetic, and indeed they are, but we forget that these grapes were pressed in the wine press of a deep agony, the heart's blood of a mother who remained faithful to the very end – a house founded on rock, stable in the midst of storms.

The House – *image of the Christian*

If we look at the empty house as image of Mary the virgin, the symbolism for ourselves is obvious. We don't have to spell out our personal need and emptiness, we know these only to well. It is an emptiness, 'a swept and dusted house', that has to be filled with God or surely it will be filled with seven devils!

We are called then to be open to the Spirit as Mary was in her virginal 'Fiat' so that we too may become fruitful, like her take on the warmth of the sun, the light of the holy lamp, become pillars of steadfast devotion for others.

When the Lord showed his mother to Julian of Norwich he said 'Can you see in her how greatly *you* are loved?' not 'Can you see in her how greatly *she* is loved?' In Mary we see how much each one is loved, individually and personally.

Richeldis' empty, unadorned wooden house was a means of bringing to the minds of pilgrims the kind of person Mary was when she uttered her 'Yes' to motherhood – a woman empty, poor, yet receptive and joyful in that poverty.

The goal of the pilgrim then is to come to her house and there to stand symbolically where Mary has stood, to utter 'yes' in the context of each one's own life, to become like Mary a house of God, a hearer of the Word and a bearer of the Spirit.

To become a similar house, another Mary, is one of the Christian's ideals. It is to be, as Sr Elizabeth of the Trinity puts it 'another humanity wherein Christ renews all his mystery'; it is to be like Mary at the Annunciation, opening oneself to the work of the Spirit who forms Christ again in the body and soul of the person who listens and adores.

At Walsingham the place of the house is venerated rather than the image because here I put myself in Mary's shoes, stand in her home at Nazareth, with her say 'Yes' and let virginity become fruitful in maternity as I welcome the Word. In doing this I become in very truth a new Nazareth, a new home for the Lord in my own person and in my own place.

So we can end with another scriptural passage which epitomises our silent abiding with Mary day by day:

When I enter my house I shall find rest with her,
for companionship with her has no bitterness
and life with her has no pain
but gladness and joy.   (Wis. 8.16)

NOTES

1. Caryll Houselander. *The Reed of God* p. 12 Sheed and Ward.
2. Dom C. Marmion *Christ in His Mysteries* p. 157 Sands and Co. 1924.
3. John Steinbeck *The Grapes of Wrath* p. 75 Guild Publishing 1979 in arrangement with W. Heinemann Ltd.
4. Ibid p. 439.

AVE MARIA GRATIA PLENA

4.   *The Annunciation*

THE mystery of the Annunciation stands in contradistinction to the symbol of the house, so that both are held in tension. The house is the image of stability. To build is to create something destined to endure beyond one's own life-span. Therefore, building is always an act of hope; it speaks of trust in the future; a certainty that there *will* be a future.

Richeldis' house perpetuates *her* memory. It symbolises the permanence of the Church enduring from generation to generation. It 'roots' Nazareth in England – now and for the years ahead: 'a perpetual memorial'.

A statue can be moved around, find a new setting at will or convenience, not so a house. It is the house that makes Nazareth permanently present in Walsingham, standing firm and strong, guaranteeing the future of the village and shrine.

But this symbol of stability is balanced by the theme of the

47

Annunciation which implies a radical openness to change and growth. Every person carries within themselves an element of unpredictability. We are not machines to be manipulated but free persons able to respond and to choose. Mary's future did not unfold as she had planned or expected, just as Walsingham's own history must surely have developed in a way Richeldis could not and did not forsee.

Richeldis gave momentum to something bigger than herself and her own private piety, just as Mary was to give birth to a Son whose future was not in her own hands All life, real life, is unpredictable. Stability should prepare us for change or it becomes mere stagnation.

It seems that the mystery of the Annunciation was particularly revered in England all through the Middle Ages. It had for centuries been the custom in Europe to ring a bell called the curfew (or 'cover fire') at sunset. Gradually this bell, often termed the 'Gabriel bell', became the signal for people to say three Hail Marys in honour of the Incarnation. These were first designated as prayers for the success of the Crusades but later the Franciscans were instrumental in propagating the evening *Aves* as a devotion in its own right, and no doubt they had a particular influence on Walsingham where a friary was established in 1347. In England however the evening salutation of Mary was extended from the customary three Aves to five, with the addition of the Lord's prayer.

At the special request of Henry IV a bell ringing was added in the morning when the same prayers were to be said, and later again at noon also. From this practice originated the Angelus, although its present form dates from after the Reformation.

In 1399 the Archbishop of Canterbury, writing to the Bishop of London and the other bishops states that 'The contemplation of the great mystery of the Incarnation in which the eternal Word chose the holy and immaculate Virgin, that from her womb he should clothe himself with flesh, has drawn all Christians to venerate her from whom arose the first beginnings of our redemption ... But we English, being the servants of her special inheritance and her Dowry, as we are commonly called, ought to surpass others in the fervour of our praises and devotions'.[1]

The actual form of the *Hail Mary* varied in medieval times and consisted only of the first half of the prayer, the angel's greeting and the words of Elizabeth. The second half 'Holy Mary mother of God, pray for us sinners now and at the hour of our death' seems to have been a much later addition.

A thirteenth century rhyming variant is as follows:

> Marie full of grace, weel de be,
> Godd of hevene be with thee,
> Oure all wimmen blisced to be
> So be the bern datt is boren of thee.[2]

The Acrene Riwle gives a form of the Ave as:

> Hail Mary, full of grace, the Lord is with thee.
> Blessed art thou among women and blessed is the fruit of thy womb. The Holy Spirit shall come upon thee, and the power of the Most High shall overshadow thee: and therefore the Holy one that shall be born of thee shall be called the Son of God. Behold the handmaid of the Lord; be it done unto me according to thy word.[3]

The Incarnation is central to Christian faith. God has become truly human through being born of a human mother. He has become one of us, like us in all things but sin. Therefore nothing human is alien to God, nothing is outside the divine sphere. In this I think we can see the significance of the 'Incarnational' aspects of pilgrimage which can shock only if we refuse to face the fact that God really *has* entered our human situation in all its messiness, that he consorts with the poor, the sick, the sinners, the outcasts of society who, lacking all spiritual sophistication and wordly cynicism, haunt places of pilgrimage hoping to touch the hem of Christ's garment.

* * *

In medieval times the feast of the Annunciation heralded the beginning of the new civil year. Everything was deemed to flow from this mystery. Yet the Incarnation came about in a way God so often enters our own lives, by a route unforseen and unexpected, as has happened throughout salvation history if we examine the Bible attentively.

For example, looking at the women of the genealogy at the beginning of St Matthew's gospel we do not find there the conventionally pious, the excellent wives and mothers, the upholders of morality as we understand it. Instead we find Tamar who, desirous of children, dresses as a prostitute and conceives by deceiving her father-in-law, Judah. We find Rahab, the professional harlot, who welcomes the Israelite spies to Jericho and hides them. Then there is Ruth, the foreign widow who marries Rahab's son Boaz and is a direct foremother of King David. There is Bathsheba, wife of Uriah the Hittite, raped by David and subsequently taken into his harem when her husband is murdered. And the genealogy ends with Mary, the supreme 'wild card', only incorporated into Joseph's Davidic inheritance by marriage when she is already pregnant, carrying a child 'conceived by the Holy Spirit' out of wedlock.

No, these are not conventional women. But the whole lesson of Scripture is that God can bring holiness, beauty, perfection from what is, humanly speaking, sinful, ugly, flawed. He works in and through human events in all their ambiguity. We see Tamar's incest and deception, Rahab's harlotry, Ruth's widowhood and foreign birth, Bathsheba's forced adultery. But there is also another side to these women. There is Tamar's courage and resourcefulness as she fights for the right to bear a child. There is Rahab's great heartedness and her ability to read the signs of the times; Ruth's loyalty and devotion, her tenderness and sense of duty. We see Bathsheba courageously accepting the inevitable, the tragedy that overtakes the physically beautiful who are used and abused yet have to make the best of it.

Mary, as she is presented to us in Luke's account of the Annunciation, is a woman of her people. She stands for the totally committed disciple; she sums up in her being all Israel's history, all its yearnings and longings, its fears and hopes. And like Israel, and the women of the genealogy mentioned above, she is called and chosen in all her human reality, simply out of love. *She* has not chosen God, rather *he* has chosen her. She is a child of grace, of choice, and so she is enabled to respond to God's initiative: 'Behold the handmaid of the Lord'. But she is not the 'obvious' choice.

As far as we know, Mary was an ordinary young woman engaged to an ordinary artisan, living in Gentile Galilee, far from the temple and the religious, law-abiding Judaens. She is a virgin, therefore without status, barren, a nobody – yet she puts herself completely at God's disposal. 'Do with me what you will'. It is God's plans that are important, not her own.

Mary is virginal in that her inmost being is all-for-God. She receives everything as pure gift. But she is completely human, completely woman, able to be tempted, to suffer, to rejoice, to die. She has her own unique personality and temperament formed by her heredity and social mileu. She too has to live by faith, not sight. She does not know the next step ahead until she must take it.

Mary is not 'woman' in the abstract, some 'eternal feminine'. Rather, like all the women of the Messianic genealogy, she is a particular woman, having to cope with her own unique amalgam of strengths and weaknesses. Was she optimistic or pessimistic by nature? sociable or reclusive? outgoing or inward-looking? practical or a dreamer? Joseph took to his home a real woman with whom he had to form a real relationship, a person with a character and personality all her own. Mary had to be open to growth and development as a human being and as a member of society, just as Jesus had to grow physically, spiritually, socially. She had to make choices, accept responsibilities and ultimately let her son choose his own way forward even when she did not understand.

Mary knew what it meant to live by faith, but she also knew what it meant to trust absolutely and to find joy in that trust, confident that God would use her for his own purposes, in his own way and in his own time.

Trust in another implies readiness to venture into the unknown, secure in a love greater than oneself and one's own tiny plans. So we see that at the centre of Walsingham is the mystery of a specific woman, Mary, who listened to God and said 'Yes' from the depths of her being, a woman who handed herself over so completely that God could fulfil his will in her. In and through her a new future was inaugurated for the human race. Pondering on the Annunciation we can see that Mary's attitude encapsulates the Christian vocation given to us all – men and women alike – to listen, to love and to bear life.

To Listen

Mary at the Annunciation is shown as the attentive one. When the angel speaks to her she is ready to respond. She takes part in the dialogue, wishing to understand the message more fully and thus be a more active recipient of the Word. 'How can this be?' Because she is attentive she is ready for the radical surrender asked of her at the moment of the Incarnation. But that is one moment picked out of many others that have led up to this point and will lead from it. She had to face a future that included bewilderment and pain. She had to ponder things in her heart. There were times when she did *not* understand, such as the time when Jesus was lost in Jerusalem at the age of twelve, or when she seemed to be addressed abruptly at Cana. There was even a time when it seemed that the relatives thought Jesus was out of his mind. Still Mary clung on, and at the end was found standing at the foot of the cross – sorrowful yet still faithful.

'Blessed are those who hear the word of God and keep it.' This is the core of discipleship – hearing and keeping the word as it is revealed to us at every moment and in every event. It means walking by faith, not sight; fostering an attentive attitude, ready for the unexpected and the challenging. But on the whole we don't want to listen and be challenged, we would rather life unfolded in a predictable manner that left us feeling in charge and able to cope.

Listening is what prayer is about – attentiveness to God. We listen, we pray, so as to hear what God has to say to us. We enter into silence, taking the focus off self in order to gaze upon him with love. But this is not the only form of attention. Any way in which we focus on others rather than self in order to give, to serve, to aid them is to cultivate an attitude of prayer. To be an alert pray-er is to hear the word addressed to us personally and respond with faith; and usually this word comes through other people or life events beyond our control.

Listening was what distinguished the prophets of the Old Testament. A true prophet did not think he knew all the answers beforehand. He had to attend to God continually:

> Each morning he wakes me to hear,
> to listen like a disciple   (Is 50.4)

This listening *each* morning means in practice attentiveness to life's demands at each moment. It cannot be confined to prayer time proper. If it meant this, most of us would be in a quandary when prayer seems blank and time to spend on it is minimal in a busy day.

We do not know if Mary was officially 'at prayer' when the angel came to her, though painters like to think so, portraying the Virgin in a church-like setting among porticos and cloisters (where she most certainly was not!) Often too she is shown meditating on the scriptures at the approach of the angelic messenger. But she could just as well have been washing clothes or cooking the dinner for all we know. Maybe she was chatting with a friend when she suddenly 'got the message' hidden in the spoken words of another.

All Christians have to be attentive in the truest sense of the word – to God, to others and to the demands of life: a husband to his wife, a mother to her child, a worker or professional person to the needs of those they serve. And to listen with Mary is to hear the answer to the question 'What is asked of me now ... in this situation ?' Not 'what am I saying to myself' (we're good at those conversations!) but 'what is *God* saying?' What is he saying in this happening, this illness, this visit from a friend, this affection, this antipathy? What is he saying in these dry prayers when I can't think a good thought?' If we truly believe God speaks to us in *all* the events of life, working *all* things for good, we will be able to say 'yes' to our lives as they unfold.

To Love

Mary is inseparable from the idea of Christian love. Listening is a sign of love and listening increases love; just as Mary had to listen, not just once or twice, but every day of her life, so that love could come to fulness in her and her initial response be completed at the cross. It was not an easy path; being 'full of grace' does not dispense from effort and suffering – either for her or for ourselves. As we experience more of God's love through the gift of grace, so the more we are summoned to greater responsibilities and obligations. No longer then can we sink into our regular torpor with a clear conscience; instead we are driven outwards to give ourselves in service and self-sacrifice.

To make love our life-project, as Mary did, means for each one to cultivate an interior virginity, an open-ness and availability to the divine. It is to have a sense of one's own integrity and eschew over-dependence on others to give one's life meaning. But conversely it is also motherliness – that attitude which allows *others* to live and grow, respecting each individual's freedom and nurturing it through affirmation and challenge according to the other's capacity.

The more we know another the more we grow to love them, and growing in knowledge is hard work. Laziness is the antithesis of love. Love always makes the effort to know more so as to love and understand more of the other. Mary had to constantly extend herself in faith, in commitment to the unfolding of the Word of God – in the flesh, in scripture, and in her daily life choices. It meant too the basic love we all have to practice and which demands a constant death to selfishness; to be patient when I want to tell someone what I really think of them, to continue with necessary work when I would rather rest, to allow others to be 'other' than myself. All this seems so trivial on one level, but without it there can be no community, no family, no personal growth. As with all things, practice makes perfect. To listen and respond lovingly to others with a sense of one's own call to both virginity and motherhood is to be a Marian person.

Even if our love is hidden within our own small environment it is never, on that account, wasted. People who love and are loved increase their capacity for love. Each of us can, if we wish, be 'love in the heart of the Church' as was St Thérèse's ideal, just as Mary's love was at the heart of Nazareth. If we look at Mary we see a committed love – strong, firm, selfless, mature. 'Be it done to me ...' I offer myself for whatever you want.

Prayer should stretch our capacity for love, enabling us to love an ever greater number of people – take all the world's sorrow and pain to our hearts. It is through the knowledge of our own weakness that we understand how vulnerable each person is, how easily wounded, how much in need of understanding. Mary is mother of mercy and compassion now, just as she was to those early pilgrims who came to Walsingham seeking healing, enabling them to give healing in their turn to a world that needed it (and still needs it) so much. Love incarnate in deed – in patience, kindness, acceptance, is the only love that really counts. The rest is mere wishful thinking.

To Bear Life
People who love are, or should be, fully alive, radiant with the Lord and therefore creative, life-bestowing persons. Mary is so fully alive because she bears life itself as the fulfilment of her 'fiat'. She is so totally given to God that in her the Word becomes flesh.

Our common Christian vocation is also to give life, to bear Jesus within us for others. We have to allow him to be formed in us, let him be conceived in us as he was in Mary. This is succinctly put in an ancient prayer to Our Lady of Walsingham which has come down to us through Erasmus:

O alone of all women, Mother and Virgin, Mother most happy, Virgin most pure. Now we, sinful as we are, come to you who are all pure. We greet you, we honour you as how we may with our humble offerings. May your Son grant us that, imitating your most holy way of life, we also by the grace of the Holy Spirit, may deserve spiritually to conceive the Lord Jesus in our inmost soul, and once conceived never to lose him. Amen.

Living fully is the result of loving and listening. In Jesus and Mary we see people fully alive, fully loving. It is great pity if religious men and women strike others as being only half alive, it is a sign that something has gone wrong. We must be woken into fulness of being, as this writer says:

> Over the years we have all unconsciously developed strategies of defence against new experience. The process begins deep in the forgotten world of our childhood, in rejections and hurts there, and become a cumulative though ill defined sense that life is not a thrill but a threat. The threatened self stiffens, withdraws, erects defences or moves aggressively against the world, and becomes formidably successful in keeping love and God at bay.
>
> It seems that Jesus was dismayed at the havoc so caused. He argued the wisdom of remaining open to experience, ready to listen, waiting to respond, because God himself comes in everything that happens. He gave assurances that people who love life and let go their hold on all that defends them from the risks of love will not be lost. They will certainly gain in knowledge of the real world, because they will not unconsciously distort the facts. They will increasingly be able to live in and with all their feelings and memories, and to live in and with themselves as thinking beings. They will like being alive. In the Christian view, when life works out in the desire for more of it and the decreasing need for defensive denial or distortion of this or that ingredient of it, 'the Lord is with thee'.[4]

We have to know how to celebrate as well as how to suffer. Look at Mary at Cana. She says 'They have no wine'. She is the first to notice and to express concern. Perhaps she had gone to fill up her own glass so she was obviously not standing around, looking dis-

approving and sipping a little iced water – or equivalent! To bear
Christ is to increase our life, not diminish it; to increase our capacity
for joy and celebration as well as for suffering and the cross.

*   *   *

To listen, to love and bear life is the vocation of Mary, the vocation
of every Christian. That is why the story of the Annunciation is the
story of each one of us.

Like Mary we are summoned to listen to God, and what do we
hear 'Do not be afraid' (and how scared we usually are) 'You are
blessed, the Lord is with you (what else is Baptism and Communion?)
Then, you have been chosen to bear Christ for others, to increase his
presence in the world (yes, you, – not just Mary or a few contempla-
tives or fanatics). Our response is usually the same as Mary's initial
reaction 'How will this come about?' And the answer of course is –
'by the power of the Holy Spirit'. It is the Spirit who will accomplish
this enfleshment of Christ in our own lives, calling some to a life of
prayer, others to the apostolate, others to family life or politics or
medicine. The sick and handicapped have their own gifts too. All
form part of the whole, each one can enflesh Christ in his or her own
sphere of influence. What matters is that Jesus be with me as he was
with Mary, growing within me through my daily choices, taking me
out of self-preoccupation to attend to others and to him.

Of course this is an ongoing process. Our Lady heard much at the
Annunciation but she still had more to hear – at the Presentation, at
Cana, at Calvary. So listening is a lifelong task, one we must under-
take with trust and humility under the Spirit's guidance. With Jesus
we should ultimately be able to say 'the world must be brought to
know that I love the Father and that I am doing exactly what the
Father has told me.' (Jn 14.31)

In this Mary can be a true model. She is a person who responded
totally, allowed God to do with her all that he wanted. When Jesus
says that his mother and brothers and sisters are those who do the
will of his father we have a glimpse into the wholeness of Mary's
self-giving, her detachment, her ability to let her son 'be' in freedom;
a glimpse too into what made Mary the woman she was. It was not
bearing Christ in the flesh that made her blessed; her real motherhood lay in her surrender to the Father's will, her 'fiat' in sorrow
and in joy, in diminishment and in fulness.

Walsingham exists to remind us of the mystery of Mary's silent surrender, her self-sacrificing love, her joy and humility in bearing and believing the Word of God. In this lies Walsingham's power and its challenge. In this too lies its open-ness to an ever new and unexpected future, because the Spirit is ultimate freedom, total unpredictability. God lives not in a 'house made with hands' but in hearts that are, with Mary, ready for *anything* – 'Be it done to me according to *your* word.'

MEDIEVAL HYMN TO OUR LADY

Of all that is so fair and bright,
Velut maris stella,
Brighter than the day is light,
Parens et puella.
I cry to thee, thou seest me,
Lady, pray thy Son for me
Tam pia,
Come in trust to thee I must
Maria.

All the world abode forlorn
Eva peccatrice.
Till our dearest Lord was born
De te genetrice.
With 'ave' passed away
Darkest night to herald day,
Salutis.
The well of grace springs for our race,
Virtutis.

Lady, flower of everything,
Rosa sine spina.
Thou bearest Jesu, heaven's king.
Gratia divina.
Thou bearest of us all the prize,
Lady, Queen of paradise,
Electa.
Maiden mild, mother with Child
Es effecta

Anon (slightly adapted)

NOTES

1. Quoted on p. 217 *Our Lady's Dowry* by T. E. Bridgett. Burns and Oates 1875.
2. Ibid p. 188.
3. *The Acrene Riwle*. Ch. 1. Rendered into English by M. B. John. Burns and Oates 1955.
4. J. Neville Ward *Five for Sorrow, Ten for Joy* p. 5 Epworth Press 1971.

5. Joy, Humility, Healing

EVEN A cursory reading of the Pynson Ballad reveals that it reverberates with the message of joy. Walsingham is to be a memorial to Mary's joy at the Annunciation, the ground and origin of all her other joys; Richeldis goes about her task of building filled with gladness; since then, people have been healed and made whole in this place and are bidden to remember Mary's joy and imitate her surrender. Lastly, England is happily termed Our Lady's Dowry on account of its new Nazareth, and Mary is invoked as the Joy of Israel, most blessed among women.

All this echoes the Lucan Gospel, where the beginning of our salvation as depicted in the Infancy narrative is permeated with joy and gladness. Mary is bidden to rejoice for the Lord is with her, she is to bear a holy child. To this invitation she assents with joy 'Oh, be it done to me'. Almost immediately we see her diffusing this joy as she visits her cousin Elizabeth and the infant John leaps in his mother's womb. Mary's song, the *Magnificat*, is nothing if not a cry of happiness, as her joy overflows in a canticle reminiscent of the woman Hannah, mother of the prophet Samuel, as she glories in her fruitfulness. It is as if Mary gathers into herself all the rejoicing of Israel's mothers down the ages knowing herself to bear within her womb the promised Messiah.

My soul magnifies the Lord, and my spirit rejoices in God my Saviour

Mary's song opens with a declaration of God's greatness and her own happiness in being chosen by him for his purposes of salvation. God is Mary's source of salvation and grace; she has nothing of herself. All is received, all is gift.

For he has looked with favour on the lowliness of his servant. Surely from now on all generations will call me blessed.

Mary chose to call herself a servant – not because she had no option, but rather because she saw that service, far from being demeaning, brings with it a sense of inner peace and freedom. Mary was not coerced into her role, she accepted it gladly as a source of blessedness – for herself and as a legacy destined to endure for others.

For the Mighty One has done great things for me, and holy is his name. His mercy is on those who fear him from generation to generation.

Mary, through being open to God in her own time and in her own place has been able to be used by him. This surrender is possible for all who choose to follow her way. God's mercy is for *everyone* who wishes, his tenderness is enduring and certain even though life inevitably has its suffering and dark side.

He has shown strength with his arm: he has scattered the proud in the thoughts of their hearts. He has brought down the powerful from their thrones and lifted up the lowly; he has filled the hungry with good things, and sent the rich away empty.

Mary is no passive, mild woman. Here she proclaims loudly and emphatically that God is on the side of the poor and oppressed. She is triumphantly joyful in her God-bearing, assuring others who are 'nobodies' like herself that God will vindicate them, bringing about a new order that is not just a back up of the *status quo*.

> *He has helped his servant Israel, in remembrance of his mercy, according to the promise he made to our ancestors, to Abraham and his descendants for ever.*

Salvation, promised at the dawn of Israel's history, is now free for all – ourselves included. And it has been made possible through the consent of a woman. Mary gives the human race a new beginning, just as Abraham and Sarah opened the way for a new beginning as progenitors of the Jewish nation.

The Magnificat, Mary's song of joy, is the direct outcome of the Incarnation. It shows her as an overwhelmingly joyful woman, even though we are aware that sorrow also awaits her. Its first intimations will be spoken of by Simeon when he tells of a sword destined to pierce her heart. For every mother, joy and sorrow are closely intertwined. Mary is no exception.

* * *

The Pynson Ballad calls the Annunciation the 'ground and origin' of Mary's joy – from it flow all her other joys because she had the happiness of bearing God in the flesh for us. She co-operates intimately with God in the mystery of redemption.

In Medieval times the English had a special devotion to the joys of Mary. It is another example of balance. Just as the house, symbol of stability, balances the theme of open-ness at the Annunication, so the emphasis on joy in medieval English spirituality offers a balance to the national character which tends to introversion and seriousness. Italians, on the other hand, while being far more extroverted and exhuberant by nature, have developed their balance by devotion to the Mother of Sorrows.

This note of joy, even in the midst of contemplating the Passion, prevails in the writings of Julian of Norwich, showing how deeply it was embedded in the religious consciousness of the English people.

> And in these three words: 'It is a joy, a bliss and an endless delight to me', there were shown three heavens. Namely, by the

words 'joy' I understood the pleasure of the Father, by the word 'bliss' the glory of the Son, and by the word 'endless delight' the Holy Spirit. The Father is pleased, the Son is glorified, the Holy Spirit takes delight. And in this I saw the third way of contemplating his blessed Passion, that is to say the joy and the bliss which make him take delight in it. For our gracious Lord showed me his Passion in five ways: the first is his bleeding head, the second is the dis-colouration of his blessed face, the third is the copious bleeding of the body through the furrows made by the scourging, the fourth is the deep drying; these four, as I have said before, concern the sufferings of the Passion; and the fifth is that which has just been shown to me about the joy and the bliss of the Passion.

For it is God's will that we truly delight with him in our salvation, and through this he wants us to be mightily comforted and strengthened. Thus he wants our soul to be joyfully occupied with the help of his grace. For we are his bliss, because in us he delights without end, and so shall we in him, with his grace. All that he does for us, has done and ever shall do, was never a cost or burden for him, nor can it be, except for the dying in our humanity, beginning at the sweet Incarnation and lasting until the blessed Rising on Eastern Morning. For that length of time did the cost and the burden endured for our redemption last, and in this deed he rejoices endlessly, as is said before.

Oh Jesus, let us truly take notice of this bliss that the blessed Trinity has in our salvation, and let us desire to have as much spiritual delight, with his grace, as is said before. That is to say, that the delight in our salvation be like the joy that Christ has in our salvation, as far as that is possible while we are here on earth.[1]

While the Trinity finds joy in the wonder of salvation accomplished, so Mary, even beneath the cross, is journeying towards endless joy. The cross is the culminating point of her life as it is for her Son, and Mary, closely involved with him in redemption, symbolises each one of us, so dearly loved, called with her to endless glory and beatitude. The first joy and the last joy of her life are one. We are not exhorted to penance and lamentation through our beholding of Mary; rather we are summoned to joy, since she images us who are likewise called to endless delight.

And with this same expression of mirth and joy, our good Lord looked down to his right side and brought to my mind where our Lady stood at the time of his Passion, and he said: 'Would you like to see her?' and this sweet word sounded as if he had said: 'I know quite well that you would like to see my blessed Mother, because after myself she is the highest joy that I could show you. She is the greatest pleasure and honour to me, and the one whom all the blessed creatures most desire to see.' And because of the unique, exalted and wonderful love that he has for this sweet maiden, his blessed Mother our Lady St Mary, he showed her bliss and her joy through this sweet word, as if he said: 'Would you like to see how I love her so that you can rejoice with me in the love that I have for her and she for me?'

And also to understand this sweet word better, our good Lord speaks in love to all people who shall be saved, as if they were one single person. By this he seemed to say: 'Do you want to see in her how much you are loved? It is for love of you that I have created her so exalted, so noble, so worthy, and this pleases me. And I wish that you too are pleased with it.' For after himself she is the most blissful sight. But here I was not taught that I should long to see her physical presence whilst I am here on earth, but rather to seek the virtues of her blessed soul: her truth, her wisdom, her love, through which I will know myself and reverently fear God.

And when our good Lord had shown me this and said this word: 'Do you want to see her?' I answered and said: 'Yes, good Lord, thanks be to you; yes good Lord, if this be your will.' I said this prayer many times and I expected to see her in bodily likeness, but I did not see her so, And Jesus showed me in this word a spiritual sight of her.

And just as I had seen her before, little and simple, so he showed her to me now exalted, noble and glorious, and more pleasing to him than all creatures. And so he wants it to be known that all who take delight in him should also take delight in her, and rejoice in the delight that he has in her and she in him.[2]

* * *

While the theme of joy found expression in the English people's devotion to the joys of Mary, it is difficult to know how much Walsingham was responsible for this development. In an era when the official liturgy of the church was in Latin it was only natural that ordinary men and women had to find spiritual nourishment in other ways that touched their own experience. A focus on the mother of God added warmth, familiarity and tenderness; for mother and child are close to the most basic emotions of life. Mary is a *sine qua non* of the Incarnation and devotion to her joys seems to have taken a variety of forms. Even the number of joys varied. It was said that devotion to Mary's seven joys was a favourite of the popular martyr Thomas à Becket. A Latin hymn attributed to him names the seven as: the Annunciation, the nativity, the adoration of the Magi, the finding in the temple, the Resurrection and the Assumption and coronation of our Lady in heaven. An ancient carol gives the joys as being the nativity, the healing of the lame, the restoration of sight to the blind, the proclamation of the word of God, the raising of the dead, the crucifixion and the Resurrection (all incidents supposed to gladden Mary). John of Gaunt left money for fifteen candles to burn in the church of the Carmelites in London in honour of Mary's fifteen joys (not named). However, in the end the number five prevailed: the Annunciation, Nativity, Resurrection, Ascension and Coronation/Assumption, as depicted in this pre-reformation poem.

> Rejoice, o virgin, Christ's mother dear,
> Which hast conceived, by hearing with ear
>   of Gabriel's salutation.
> Rejoice, because to God thou art lief
> and barest Him, without pain or grief,
>   in chaste conversation.
> Rejoice, because thy most dear Son,
> whom thou didst see through the heart run,
>   rose with manifestation.
> Rejoice, because He ascended plain
> Before they face into heaven again,
>   By His proper excitation.
> Rejoice, because thou followest Him,

Opposite: (top) Interior of Slipper Chapel (© R.C. Shrine); (bottom) View of Slipper Chapel and R.C. Shrine (© R.C. Shrine).

and great honour to thee is given
in the heavenly habitation:
Where the fruit of thy womb everlasting
we may behold through thy deserving
in joy without mutation.[3]

Possibly the number five was preferred and propagated to corre-
spond with the parallel devotion to the five wounds (which also
contained a note of joy rather than sorrow).

In East Anglia especially, the Annunciation was the dominant
mystery commemorated in numerous stained glass windows, while
the honouring of Mary's five joys, together with the Lord's five
wounds, found its way into a number of wills. Candles referred to
as 'gaudes' (after the Latin *gaude* – rejoice) and possibly decorated
with flowers in honour of Mary's joys, and strings of *gaude* beads for
counting the Aves of her Salutation may well have given rise to the
term being used in reference to anything nicely decorated for joyous
purposes until, by a process of modification, 'gaudy' became an
adjective referring to anything bright or showy.

'I give half an acre of land to endow in perpetuity five gaudes
burning before our Lady in the chancel of St John the Baptist, at
every antiphon of our Lady and at Masses on the same feasts'[4]
writes a Norfolk yeoman in his will. Another, John Barnet of Bury,
Suffolk, bequeathes money for five men clad in black in honour of
the Lord's five wounds, and five women clad in white in honour of
Our Lady's five joys, to attend his requiem and internment carrying
'candles of clean wax'. John Goselyn asks for five candles each in
honour of the five wounds and the five joys to burn on his grave
during Mass on holy days.[5]

The chapter on daily devotions in the *Ancrene Riwle* devotes quite
a large amount of space to the remembrance of Mary's joys, of
which I give a slightly shortened and modified version here.

O Lady St Mary, because of the great joy you experienced
within you when Jesus, true God and son of God took flesh and
blood in you after the angel's greeting, receive my greeting

*Opposite: (top left) Pilgrimage of Crosses; (top right) Lighting Candles in the
Anglican holy house (photos: Louis Quail); (bottom) Interior of Holy Spirit
Chapel (© R.C. Shrine).*

with the same Ave, and let me make little of outward joy. Give me rather interior comfort and let me know the joys of heaven through your merits.

O Lady St Mary, because of the great joy you experienced when you saw your blessed child born from your pure body for the salvation of humankind without any breaking of virginity ... Heal me who am broken ... and grant that I may see your blessed face in heaven.

O Lady St Mary, because of the great joy you experienced when you saw your dear and precious Son after his grievous death rise to joyful life, his body sevenfold brighter than the sun, grant me to die with him and to rise in him ... to share his sufferings as a companion on earth that I may be a companion of his in the happiness of heaven.

O Lady St Mary, because of the great joy you experienced when you saw your fair and blessed Son rising on Ascension Thursday in such glory and power to the happiness of his heavenly kingdom, grant that I may, with him, cast all the cares of the world underfoot and rise now in heart,

> at my death in spirit,
> and bodily on the day of judgement,
> to the joys of heaven.

O Lady St Mary, because of the great joy that filled all the earth when he received you into eternal happiness and with his blessed arms set you on your throne, with a queen's crown on your head brighter than the sun ... receive these greetings from me here on earth that I may greet you with happiness in heaven.

Rejoice O mother of God Immaculate Virgin!
Rejoice in the gladness you received from the angel!
Rejoice because you have brought forth the brightness of
     eternal light!
Rejoice O Mother!
Rejoice O holy mother of God!
You alone are mother and virgin.
All the creatures of your Son praise you, the mother of light.
Be for us a gracious mediatrix.
Rejoice O virgin!

Rejoice O mother of God!
Rejoice O Mary, joy of all the faithful!
Let the church rejoice without ceasing in your praises,
and make us, O loving lady, to rejoice with you before the Lord.

*   *   *

Together with the theme of joy the first chapters of St Luke's gospel
embody the concept of the *anawim* – the humble and poor of Israel;
such men and women as Zachary and Elizabeth, Mary and Joseph,
the shepherds, Simeon and Anna. Mary herself lives in an ambience
redolent of humility. She is portrayed as a humble woman in an
ordinary village; she gives birth among the poor and dispossessed
at Bethlehem; she knows the disorientation and vulnerability attendant on being an exile and refugee among strangers in Egypt.

It is humility, being rooted in the truth of her creature-hood and
dependence on God, that enables Mary to accept and rejoice in the
vocation offered to her, and voiced in the *Magnificat*.

Only the humble can really be grateful, realising as they do that
everything is gift – undeserved and unmerited. It is only when we
realise this that we can be happy with what we have received, rather
than being resentful at what we have been denied.

Everything at Walsingham speaks of humility; the empty house
waiting, the poor who come for healing, those who are humble
enough to forget self and rejoice in the mystery of Mary's joy at the
Incarnation. This is to live in the world of gospel faith where each
person is assured of being loved, accepted, tenderly cherished and
fully redeemed, whatever their sins or natural disabilities.

Humility is the Marian virtue singled out by the Pynson Ballad. It
is a word derived from 'humus' – soil. Our Lady is presented as a
woman of the land, earthly and ordinary. And it is humility which
disposes the poor for healing. They know their need; but they come
to Walsingham not only to ask for help but to be joyful. Joy has an
inherent power to heal. Just to be with other sick people makes the
infirm realise their own blessings, drawing them out of self in order
to be concerned with others.

To come to the holy house, just as one is, needy, suffering, in pain,
is to have a claim on Mary's maternal heart. It is to come within the
circle of four walls, held, enclosed, 'enfolded in love' as Julian
would say. It is this security which enables the pilgrim to echo

Mary's 'fiat' – to say yes to God in all his or her weakness and woundedness. When we can be secure enough to say 'yes' with Mary then healing can take place at our deepest level. Only when we are 'at home' – welcomed, loved, accepted, can we open ourselves to life with a sense of security and trust.

*   *   *

One of the features of Walsingham in the past seems to have been the presence of holy wells. Their origin is uncertain. They are mentioned in the Pynson Ballad as 'twin wells'; but later tradition speaks of their having healing qualities. Erasmus writes:

> There were a couple of wells (under that house) both full of water to the brink, and they say that the spring of those wells is dedicated to our Lady, that the water is very cold and medicinal for headaches and heartburn. They say that the fountain suddenly sprang up from the earth at the command of our Lady.

Lady wells, water associated with a Marian shrine and claiming healing properties were relatively common. Their symbolism is obvious – cleansing, new birth, new life for those who approach with faith. Today the restored Anglican Shrine has its own holy well, and the Slipper Chapel too has its water fountain. Healing and cleansing are part of pilgrimage whether there is an external miracle or not.

In Medieval England, the lack of medical knowledge meant that for many people the hope of healing could only come from prayer and pilgrimage. Even now there is much that is outside the sphere of conventional medicine. Walsingham still has its cures and miracles but by far the greater number of healings are interior – healings of the pain and disfigurement we all bear in one way or another, and which can only be touched by a power of love beyond ourselves when we are humble, open and expectant. A Lady well, so simply recalled in this poem by an Anglican clergyman is a symbol that still speaks to us whether we seek a miracle or not.

THE LADY'S WELL
It flow'd like light from the voice of God,
Silent and calm and fair;

It shone where the child and the parent trod
  in the soft and evening air.

Look at that spring, my father dear,
  where the white blossoms fell:
Why is it always bright and clear?
  And why the Lady's well?

Once on a time, my own sweet child,
  there dwelt across the sea
a lovely Mother, meek and mild,
  from blame and blemish free.

And Mary was her blessed name,
  in every land adored:
Its very sound deep love should claim
  from all who love their Lord.

A child was hers – a heavenly birth,
  as pure as pure could be:
He had no father of the earth,
  The Son of God was He.

He came down to her from above,
  He died upon the Cross;
We never can do for Him, my love,
  what He hath done for us.

And so to make His praise endure,
  because of Jesus's fame,
Our fathers called things bright and pure
  by His fair Mother's name.

She is the Lady of the well –
  Her memory was meant
with lily and with rose to dwell
  by waters innocent.

(R. S. Hawker)

Joy, humility, healing. All are part of the story of Walsingham and
all are connected to the Annunciation at their root – the desire to say
'yes' to God with Mary and thus be open to all God asks in a spirit
of joyful trust. This alone can salve the deep wounds of the human

spirit. Mary – all pure, limpid as water reflecting the light of God in her soul and in her body, is totally at one with God as she invites us into that mystery also by way of humility, gratitude and joy.

NOTES

1. Julian of Norwich op.cit. ch. 23.
2. Ibid ch. 25.
3. From a Prymer of 1538; Maskell, Monum. Rit. ii. p. 74 Quoted in Bridgett op.cit. p. 67
4. From *Blomefield's History of Norfolk* i p. 273 Quoted in Bridgett op.cit. p.65
5. Ibid p. 67.

6. Pilgrimage

WHY DID the men and women of medieval England go on pilgrimage and why has the custom endured and indeed been revived during the present time? Maybe it is because pilgrimage seems to answer a deep need in human nature. It is a way to externalise what we know interiorly – that life itself is a journey in time, and time never stands still. We are borne along on its stream whether we will or no.

In the Judaeo – Christian tradition time is not cyclical and meaningless, it is linear. Time is sacred. God reveals himself gradually to Israel over the passage of time and ultimately enters into time himself in the Incarnation. God has become part of human history.

Life is also characterised by movement – no life means no movement; and as life itself is a journey so there is in human consciousness a certain restlessness, a desire to travel, to encounter new places, new people; or to see old or personally significant places through new eyes: linking past and present, finding one's family or national or religious roots. Memory is the source of our self-identity; the more complete our memory the better the knowledge we have of who we are and what direction our lives should take in the future. To be linked with our past, consciously, is to remember continually, even as we face the future.

Sacred places, places of significance for our faith, have their biblical prototype in the pilgrimage that the ancient Israelites used to make to Jerusalem. Jerusalem held a unique place spiritually and symbolically ever since it was first decreed that the Jewish people should 'present themselves there before the Lord' on major religious festivals, especially Passover, which commemorated the wanderings of the Israelites in the desert and their final entry into the promised land.

Jerusalem was considered to be God's specially chosen city. Not only had it been the capital of a united country under David, it was the city of the temple, where the pilgrims felt themselves to be standing before the Lord in his own courts. Jerusalem was holy, embodying the religious and national aspirations of Judaism. Joy at the sight of Jerusalem filled the pilgrims approaching the city from the Mount of Olives when they saw the golden dome of Herod's temple glistening in the sunshine. In prophecy Jerusalem was to be a city sacred to the Lord for all nations:

> The foreigners who join themselves to the Lord, to minister to him, to love the name of the Lord, and to be his servants, all who keep the Sabbath and do not profane it, and hold fast my covenant – these I will bring to my holy mountain, and make them joyful in my house of prayer; their burnt offerings and their sacrifices will be accepted on my altar; for my house shall be called a house of prayer for all peoples. Thus says the Lord God, who gathers the outcasts of Israel, I will gather others to them besides those already gathered.   (Is. 56.8–8)

Finally, Jerusalem is to be the 'city without walls', so vast is her populace. God alone is her protector and glory:

> Jerusalem shall be inhabited like villages without walls, because of the multitude of people and animals in her. For I will be a wall of fire round about her, says the Lord, and I will be the glory within her. The Lord will inherit Judah as his

portion in the Holy Land, and will again choose Jerusalem. (Zech. 2.4, 5, 12)

Luke's gospel narrative revolves around Jerusalem. His story begins with the priest Zechariah in the temple. It continues with the Presentation, when Mary brings the Child to be presented before the Lord and Simeon utters his canticle of praise, naming Jesus as light of the nations and glory of Israel. We are told that Mary and Joseph went annually to the temple at Passover, and when Jesus was twelve years old he accompanied his parents and showed his consciousness of his emerging identity. A great part of the body of Luke's gospel is concerned with Jesus making his final journey to Jerusalem where his crucifixion and resurrection are to take place; and this journey reaches a climax mid-way when Jesus weeps over the city he loves, aware of what the future holds in store for it:

> Jerusalem, Jerusalem, the city that kills the prophets and stones those who are sent to it! How often have I desired to gather your children together as a hen gathers her brood under her wings, and you were not willing! See your house is left to you. And I tell you, you will not see me until the time comes when you say, 'Blessed is the one who comes in the name of the Lord'. (Lk 13.34–35)

After the Ascension Luke shows us the disciples returning to Jerusalem with great joy 'and they were continually in the temple blessing God' (Lk 24.53), while the book of Acts opens in the same city where the disciples, with Mary the mother of Jesus and other women, are gathered in prayer. The coming of the Spirit at Pentecost then sets off a worldwide movement beginning at Jerusalem and from there spreading to the ends of the known world through Paul's missionary journeys.

Even after its destruction by Titus following an heroic defence, Jerusalem continued to be a centre of longing for Jews and Christians alike. Every year at Passover, the Jew of the Diaspora would hope to celebrate the festival 'next year in Jerusalem'. Centres of Rabbinic learning were established as close as possible to the holy city, and the wailing wall, all that was left of Herod's temple, received the Jews' murmured petitions for a return to Sion, and their notes and prayers were stuffed into its cracks and crevices.

For Christians, the pull towards Jerusalem was due to the desire to see the holy places connected with the life of Christ, to pray at the Sepulchre of the resurrection and follow the way of the cross. The Crusades were initiated specifically to re-open the holy land for pilgrims, enabling them to venerate the sites so dear to their faith. To go to Jerusalem was considered the high point of a life and/or a fitting way to inaugurate a decisive step of conversion; so it was for St Francis, for St Ignatius, and nearer our own time, Charles de Foucauld.

Jerusalem is far more than a city. It has a unique symbolic role and the power to activate deep emotions. H. V. Morton writes graphically of a pilgrim he encountered at the holy sepulchre during his own journey through the holy land in the first part of this century.

At home one always thinks of Jesus in heaven, on the right hand of God the Father ... As God, He is everywhere, but in Jerusalem centuries of piety have competed to place His footsteps on this stone and that road. It was almost with a shock that I realised that the Via Dolorosa could be a real road with men and women and animals upon it.

Only two, or at the most, three people can enter the Sepulchre at one time. On the right hand is a cracked slab of white marble, three feet in height, covering the rock on which He was placed after the Crucifixion.

I could see a pilgrim kneeling at the Sepulchre, so I waited in the small, dark ante-chamber outside. Becoming impatient, I bent down and, peeping through the low entrance, saw that the man inside was an old, bent peasant in ragged clothes, his feet in a pair of huge shoes made of felt, who had come over in a pilgrim ship, as the Russians used to come, and he had probably been saving up all his life for that moment.

His large rough hands, the nails split and black with labour, touched the marble gently with a smoothing motion; then he would clasp them in prayer and cross himself.

He prayed aloud in a trembling voice, but I could not understand what he was saying. Then, taking from his pocket various pieces of dirty paper and a length of ribbon, he rubbed them gently on the Tomb and put them back in his pocket.

I thought there might perhaps be room for me, so I bent my head and entered the Sepulchre. The Greek monk, the kneeling peasant and myself quite filled the small space. And it would have been all right if the old man had continued to kneel, but, disturbed perhaps by my entrance, he rose up, the tears still falling, and whispered something to me. We were now standing, our chests touching, and, looking into his eyes, I realised that I was looking at real happiness ... I would have given the world to have been able to speak to him, but we stood there in the Tomb of Christ, he whispering something to me which I did not understand, and I shaking my head.

The old man sank down on his knees and turned again to the Tomb, unwilling to leave, incoherent with faith and devotion, his big, scarred hands touching the marble lovingly as if stroking the hair of a child. Presently he backed out of the candle-light into the dim Chapel of the Angel.[1]

While the first choice of the medieval pilgrim was Jerusalem, an actual journey to the Holy Land was not always, indeed not usually, possible. The distance was prohibitive in an age of slow and dangerous travel; it was expensive to pay the necessary fares and there was also the uncertain political situation. So there grew up other places of pilgrimage for those unable to travel to Palestine and walk in the actual footsteps of Christ: places such as Rome and Canterbury made holy by the blood of martyrs, or places which boasted some special relics like those of St James at Compostella or the holy coat at Trier. In fact nearly every large church and cathedral possessed a quota of relics, sometimes taken as part of the spoils of war. Through these artefacts people hoped to have access to a portion of heaven-on-earth.

The veneration of relics was closely tied to a belief in the reality of the Incarnation. In Christ God had become man, had walked on earth, eaten our food, known the experience of a mother and home, knew what it was to be rejected, to weep, to suffer, to die. His cross, his clothes, were precious reminders of his closeness to our earth. Others, the saints, were revered because of their nearness to him, their lives which reflected his presence and power. By the time of the second council of Nicea in 787 it was stated that no new church could be consecrated without relics, they were considered an essential part of the altar. Walsingham had not only its holy house but

also, according to Erasmus, a fine collection of relics housed in a
special chapel, including an enormous bone, reputed to be the fin-
ger joint of St Peter, and a vial of our Lady's milk, a chalky substance
which was often gathered up from the cave of the nativity in
Bethlehem and mixed with a little liquid.

Many other artefacts brought the Holy Land to Europe – the true
cross, the crown of thorns (for which St Louis built the Sainte
Chappelle) the holy coat, the holy shroud, the virgin's girdle, and in
England the Holy Blood of Hailes. It is hardly necessary to state that
this multiplication of relics gave rise to a number of abuses, but
underneath there remained the valid desire of the human heart to be
in contact with the transcendant reality all these things symbolised.
Pilgrimages to holy places were genuine manifestations of popular
piety – the piety of the 'all sorts' for whom theology 'proper' had no
appeal. Pilgrims from every walk of life were like the crowds who
thronged around our Lord during his lifetime, hoping for a word, a
look, a sign of love, an assurance that they were, despite everything,
valuable and worthwhile.

In the Holy Land itself pilgrims went literally to a *place* rather
than a statue or relic but there were other places nearer home to
visit, for example the hermitage of St Guthlac in Lincolnshire, the
Isle of Iona, the abbey of St Etheldreda at Ely. To go to such places
was to bridge the gap between the sacred and secular world, to
experience a new sense of continuity and belonging. It was not just
belief in the abstract. Pilgrims could *see* the building, *touch* the relics,
hear the chanting of monastic choirs whose communities guarded
and adorned the sacred precincts.

There were many motives for a man or woman to go on pilgrimage. There was the very natural desire to travel and broaden one's
life experience in a time when holidays and tourism in the modern
sense were unknown. A pilgrimage might be undertaken as fulfilment of a vow or to mark a new stage of life. It might be a form of
retribution; for example, sometimes a judge would order a criminal
to go to a distant shrine, thus removing him from the scene of his
crime and giving the opportunity for a spiritual experience. A priest
might likewise enjoin pilgrimage as a penance when a serious sin
was confessed. Those who did not wish to go themselves could fulfil their obligation by engaging a substitute who went on behalf of
the person concerned. Pilgrimages were not grim occasions even
though the journey had its hardships. There was a holiday atmos-

phere with singers and pipers in attendance. There would be nobles with their retinues, poorer folk on foot. Travel was slow, with frequent stops at churches, inns and religious houses en route.

With the passage of time the Church began to insist that those going on a pilgrimage should obtain approval from the bishop. This meant that, before setting out, intending pilgrims would gather at a designated church for a blessing, wearing the pilgrim garb which consisted of a long smock with a hood, a staff, and a large hat. The word 'palmers' was coined for those who returned with palms from the Holy Land, and was later, broadened as a term to include all pilgrims. Each shrine had its particular symbol which could henceforth be worn with pride. A cockle shell signified a completed pilgrimage to Compostella. Walsingham seems to have favoured badges depicting the Annunciation, while other shrines issued leather flasks to hold water from holy wells and sacred springs.

After Jerusalem, Nazareth was considered the most sacred place for Christians to visit. But it too was far away, inaccessible. In Nazareth the Word had become flesh in the womb of the Virgin and at Nazareth Jesus had grown from childhood to manhood. His eyes had rested upon its encircling hills covered with bright anemones in springtime, and from the crest of these same hills he could glimpse the Mediterranean sea sparkling on the horizon beyond the peaks of Mount Carmel. While Jerusalem in Judea was the city of his passion, Nazareth in Galilee was his home and the village containing his mother's house. Here Mary had conceived him by the power of the Holy Spirit, and here Jesus had advanced in age and wisdom, surrounded by family and friends, until the time came for him to commence his public ministry and move away. Nazareth symbolised for Jesus security, home, the growing ears which saw him develop into the man who knew himself to be Son of the Eternal Father yet fully human.

So for England to have its own Nazareth in the form of Richeldis' holy house was considered a special joy and honour. We can surmise how those medieval pilgrims must have felt as they went through the Priory gateway and their eyes rested upon the beautiful church of grey flint, inset with intricate patterns, every cornice holding the statue of a saint, every window filled with coloured glass that, when seen from inside, set the building alight with splendour. The nave of the great church was hung with rich silks and velvets, displaying banners sent to commemorate victorious battles and silver images of knights mounted on their chargers. The choir, set apart for the canons, was divided off from the main body of the church by an ornately carved rood screen, and the window over the high altar depicted the Annunciation and was flanked by images of St Edward the Confessor, St Catherine, St Margaret and St Edmund. To the right of the altar a vial said to contain some of our Lady's milk was guarded by a canon, with a collecting plate nearby for alms.

The holy house itself was enclosed in a special chapel. The *novum opus* or 'new work' that surrounded it was still in process of construction when Erasmus visited the shrine. Windows had not yet been installed, leaving the place cold and draughty. No doubt many pilgrims were glad of the air when numbers of people were pushing themselves forward in a suffocatingly small place.

The pilgrims mounted a few steps and there before them stood Richeldis' Nazareth chapel in the form of a little house made of wood. On entering it they encountered a dark interior lit only by a blaze of candles and silver lamps, with more silks and fine cloth covering the walls. On the altar, to one side, was the famous image of our Lady of Walsingham. If the wax seal of the Priory is correct, the original image showed Mary with the Child on her lap. Erasmus calls it a small statue 'excelling neither in material nor workmanship'. Mary sits on a high backed throne, the top of which is semi-circular, and beneath her feet is a greenish translucent toadstone, an East Anglian symbol of evil, showing that she had 'trodden all filthiness, malice and pride beneath her'. The Child on her lap carries the book of the Gospels and in Mary's right hand is a lily sceptre. The seal also depicts curtain-like drapes drawn back to reveal the image, and it is possible that the statue was kept behind these for at least part of the time (as was the famous crucifix of Burgos in Spain). If so, it could mean that the statue kept some of its original colour and did not darken like the black Virgin of Montserrat. Nearby, another canon hovered, ready to collect offerings in the Virgin's name, while the pilgrims filed through the holy house and out by another door.

From thence they proceeded to the holy wells and to the nearby chapel of St Lawrence where more relics could be seen in a wooden shed which seems to have had a bearskin tacked to one wall! Erasmus even mentions being shown a fragrant branch on which it was said the Virgin had sat, but of the story which gave rise to this legend there is no trace.

One of the attractions of pilgrimage was the possibility of gaining what was called an 'indulgence'. This practice, when understood correctly, was an entirely valid interpretation of the Christian doctrine of the communion of saints. While the church could, and did in its early days, ask people to perform severe penances for sin, so she could give generously from the store of holiness that was hers on account of Christ and his saints. Instead of so many days of fasting, for example, the church offered an alternative means of making reparation – special prayers, or a visit to a shrine. An 'indulgence' was, as its name suggests, an offer of mercy instead of 'exacting the last farthing'.

The greatest (or plenary) indulgence, was attached to those who, as crusaders or pilgrims, travelled to the Holy Land. For this the church offered a total remission of sins because she considered this journey a mark of outstanding love, risking even life itself to walk in the places sanctified by Christ's earthly presence.

St Francis, that great champion of the common people, knew that few could go so far. It is a well authenticated tradition that he therefore asked the pope to attach to the little chapel of the Portiuncula, cradle of the Franciscan Order and dedicated to our Lady of the Angels, a plenary indulgence on the anniversary of its consecration, August 2nd. Those who visited the chapel would then be blessed as fully as if they had actually gone to Jerusalem. The Portiuncula, like Walsingham, is a 'house within a house', the tiny chapel now cradled within a great basilica. In no time at all word spread that a special indulgence was offered there every year. Crowds beseiged the place. The idea spread and soon other shrines gained similar privileges.

One of the most famous pilgrims to Assisi was the mystic and penitent Angela of Foligno. Angela was born during the lifetime of St Clare and was therefore very close to the sources of early Franciscan spirituality.

All we know of Angela's life (which is not much) is found in the Prologue and text of her book. Brother Arnold, her confessor, writes that Angela was a married laywoman with a husband and many children; she was rich but uneducated and not physically strong. Her family, including her mother, were still living when Angela, touched by grace, determined to live a more dedicated Christian life. However, during the first years of her conversion they all died (maybe from fever or plague) leaving her alone, free to pursue her relationship with God as she chose. Under the guidance of the friars at Foligno, Angela professed the rule of a Franciscan Tertiary and gradually abandoned a social and public life, living simply with a companion, 'a virgin who accompanied her in her travels and in her works of mercy'.

To mark the stage of her final conversion and to beg the grace of henceforth living in perfect poverty, Angela made a pilgrimage to Rome and then to Assisi where the newly built basilica of St Francis dominated the approach to the city. Her account of the ascent is one of the most poignant in religious literature, a fitting end to one era of Angela's life and the beginning of another. She writes:

> Whilst then I was journeying along and praying ... just as I had arrived between the cave and the narrow path which leads up to Assisi, and a little beyond the cave; in that place it was said to me: 'You have asked of my servant Francis, and I have been pleased to send another messenger. I am the Holy Spirit who have come to give you consolation such as you would never otherwise have tasted. And I will come with you inwardly as far as St Francis' Church, and some of those who are with you will notice my presence a little. And it is my will to come with you and to speak with you the whole of the way, and I will not cease speaking, nor will you be able to listen to anything else apart from me ...'
>
> Then he began to say to me the following words to provoke me to love him: 'O my sweet daughter! O my daughter, my temple! O my daughter my delight! Love me because you are greatly loved by me, much more than I am loved by you!' And often he said to me 'O my daughter and sweet spouse!' And he added in an underbreath 'I love you more than any woman in the valley of Spoleto ...'
>
> And it came to pass the second time when I came to the Church of St Francis, that when I knelt down straight-away at the door of the church and saw the painting representing St Francis in the bosom of Christ, Christ said to me: 'Thus will I hold you closely in my embrace, and much more closely than can be seen with any bodily eyes. And now this is the hour when I will fill you, my sweet daughter, my temple, my delight, and will let you go. For I told you that so far as this consolation is concerned I leave you, but otherwise I will never leave you

while you love me.' And although it was a bitter word, nevertheless in the very word itself I felt such great sweetness that it was most delightful. And then I looked that I should see him with the eyes of my body and my soul, and I saw him. And if you ask me what I saw, know that I saw something real and true, full of majesty, immense, I know not what; but it seemed to me that it was good.

Moreover he spoke many words of sweetness to me. And in withdrawing from me he made a very peaceful departure, and he went away with immense sweetness, and he went away openly and slowly, and not suddenly.

And among other words he spoke these to me: 'My sweet daughter, more sweet to me than I to you, my beloved temple; you have the ring of my love and you are espoused by me. And in the future you should not depart from me, and you have the blessing of the Father, and of the Son, and of the Holy Spirit, as does your companion too.'[2]

What a gift it would have been if some English woman such as Julian of Norwich, Angela's near-contemporary, had written something of her personal experience of a pilgrimage of Walsingham had she made one at a similar turning point in her own life. But there we can only conjecture; the records are silent, and Julian may never have ventured further than her own city, whose cathedral possessed the tomb of Little Saint William.

While pilgrimage could be for some a valid religious experience, in the later Middle Ages there were definitely abuses. The doctrine of indulgences was a cause of scandal as it became less understood and more open to monetary abuse. Relics multipled at a rate that produced incredulity and cynicism. People of education like Erasmus were rightly questioning the richness of shrines and the improbability of many artefacts. But pilgrimage itself was never called into question for the concept is deeply rooted in the Incarnation and appeals to all kinds of people. It embodies the need to be close to God and his saints, to be made new and to be healed through contact with the holy. And in finding God in a specific place at the end of a specific journey the pilgrim is encouraged to find him everywhere – including home – where he has been indeed all the time!

NOTES

1 p. 8–12 *In the Steps of the Master*. H. V. Morton. Methuen 1934.
2. p. 56, 57 *The Visions and Instructions of Blessed Angela of Foligno*. Translated by a secular priest. Richardson 1871 (Translation adapted).

7. *Restoration and Renewal*

It is perhaps only natural to lament the overthrow of the medieval shrine of our Lady of Walsingham, but surely, like the destruction of Jerusalem of old, this devastation had a purifying effect.

> How lonely sits the city that once was full of people!
> How like a widow she has become,
> She that was great among the nations!
> She that was a princess among the provinces has become a
>   vassal.
> She weeps bitterly in the night,
> with tears on her cheeks;
> among all her lovers she has no-one to comfort her;
> All her friends have dealt treacherously with her,
> they have become her enemies.   (Lam I.1, 2)

Walsingham, like ravaged Jerusalem slept among the ruins.

The loss of the original holy house and statue was certainly irreparable, yet can we really regret the passing of such a place as Walsingham seems to have become by the time of the monastic suppression? So much wealth, so many questionable relics, so many pilgrims of dubious repute, plus all the abuses attendant on a religious community that has an overabundance of life's good things.

> What can I say for you, to what compare you,
> O daughter of Jerusalem?
> To what may I liken you that I may comfort you,
> O virgin daughter Sion?
> For vast as the sea is your ruin; who can heal you?
> Your prophets have seen for you false and deceptive visions;
> they have not exposed your iniquity to restore your fortunes,
> but have seen oracles for you
> that are false and misleading.   (Lam. 2.13, 14)

It would seem that Walsingham needed the break to recover her simplicity, her true message for England and for the world; for what is now at Walsingham is a development and completion of the past in the best sense.

> For a brief moment I abandoned you,
> but with great compassion I will gather you.
> In overflowing wrath for a moment I hid my face from you,
> but with everlasting love I will have compassion on you,
> says the Lord, your Redeemer.   (Is 54.7, 8)

Like the Jews returning to their holy city after the exile, Walsingham holds a purified message of comfort, hope and reconciliation. She has arisen as a phoenix from the fire. There is a new resurgence of prayer, peace, understanding, based not on an ornate edifice but on the simplicity and humility that are born of respect for others; and there is a far deeper ecumenical alliance between Anglican and Roman Catholic shrines than would have seemed possible even a few years ago. This is far more in keeping with Mary's original desire to make of Walsingham England's Nazareth – a home with a welcome for all.

The steadfast love of the Lord never ceases,
his mercies never come to an end;
they are new every morning; great is your faithfulness …
For the Lord will not reject forever.
Although he causes grief, he will have compassion
according to the abundance of his steadfast love.

(Lam 3.22, 23, 31, 32)

After the dissolution, who or what Walsingham was about seems to have been confined to near-oblivion. The English people on the whole became part of the newly established English church which did not encourage or revere shrines and statues. Many beautiful churches were denuded of their statuary, wall paintings were defaced and rood screens removed. Norfolk, due to its long association with the Protestant Low Countries, tended towards Puritanism and nonconformity, although a few Catholic families who had sufficient money to pay the necessary fines attendant on recusancy managed to survive here and there.

With Catholic Emancipation in 1829 devotion to our Lady tended to be of the 'imported' variety, fostered by immigrant priests – Irish, Italian, French, Spanish. Even English priests, trained abroad for the most part, gave no thought to our Lady of Walsingham; she remained only a vague legend. A book by Fr Bridgett, a Redemptorist priest, published in 1875 and treating of England as the Dowry of Mary, can say little more about Walsingham than:

Walsingham Parva was a village or small town a few miles from the sea-coast in the north of Norfolk.

The priory of Walsingham was founded between 1146 and 1174, during the episcopate of William, Bishop of Norwich.

It originated with Geoffrey de Favarches, who granted to Edwy, his clerk, the chapel which his mother, Richeldis, had built at Walsingham. Edwy was required to institute or bring in a religious order, and the priory was served by regular canons of St Augustine.

The chapel which Richeldis had built was dedicated in honour of the ever-virgin Mary; but with a reference to a MS register, Blomefield, the historian of Norfolk, asserts that she built it in obedience to a vision, or that it was intended to represent the holy house of Nazareth.

As the records of the shrine and of all the miracles worked there were destroyed by Henry, we are ignorant of how Walsingham first became a place of pilgrimage. It was so at an early date after its foundation.[1]

The writer knows of the famous statue of Our Lady but can give no description of it; and he writes as if that, rather than the house, was most important. In his day Our Lady of Walsingham belonged only to history books, and even then in a garbled version.

Travel writers of 1927 and 1930, H. V. Morton and M. R. James respectively, offer their readers only the vaguest idea of Walsingham's origins, assuring the public that the house of Nazareth was said to have been transported there from the holy land by angels as in the legend of the *sancta casa* of Loreto.[2] Both refer to the devotion as being of merely historical interest, having no relevance to the present day. James notes that the Slipper Chapel is well restored and in the care of Benedictines, though no service is ever held in it. He mentions nothing about any resurgence of pilgrimages or devotion to Mary in the area, although under Fr Hope Patten these had already begun in a small way.

The ruins of Walsingham's Augustinian priory, which came to be known (erroneously) as 'the Abbey', had been, since the early seventeenth century, in the possession of the Lee-Warner family. Bishop John Warner of Rochester acquired the property from the Earl of Leicester in 1633 and when he died childless the estate passed to his nephew, Archdeacon John Lee, son of the bishop's sister, who adopted the name Lee-Warner. Until this century when Sir Eustace Gurney married Miss Agatha Lee-Warner, the estate continued with a Lee-Warner as squire in the big house, while the remains of the priory Church and its monastic building fell into decay.

The Oxford Movement, which flourished in the mid-nineteenth century, saw a spiritual revival in the Church of England, which began to re-examine and reaffirm its Catholic heritage. Religious life was revived, new Orders founded, and forms of worship introduced which once more made use of coloured vestments, incense, candles, paintings and statues. With this went a fascination with monastic ruins and other relics of the past.

The incumbent squire, the Revd D. H. Lee-Warner, was motivated at this point to take an interest in the old priory he had inherited, parts of which remained above ground in his park; and in 1853 his nephew, Revd James Lee-Warner and Mr Henry Harrod F.S.A. excavated and mapped out what they could of the ground plan of the original buildings. The excavation showed the foundations of a great church, (extensively rebuilt in the fourteenth century) with aisles and a central tower, while the holy house was presumed to have been preserved in a special shrine chapel with very thick stone walls attached to the main Church. It seemed that the wooden house was mounted on a platform above ground level, so pilgrims would have to go up a few steps to reach the flooring of Purbeck marble on which it stood. While the actual site of the holy house was only an educated guess, later to be challenged by Fr Hope Patten, a second and more thorough excavation in 1961 proved the truth of the Lee-Warner assumption, especially as a stone coffin, found directly under the house, was acknowledge to hold the remains of Sir Bartholomew Burghesh who had directed in his will that the holy house was to be his burial place.

The Revd J. Lee-Warner was also responsible for the publication in an archeological Journal of the seal of Walsingham priory, taken from the white wax appended to the Act of Supremacy. On one side is seen a turreted church with central tower and three heads of people at prayer in three appertures. On the other side is a picture

Seal of Walsingham Priory.

presumed to be of the famous statue. Our Lady sits on a high backed throne, the Child on her knee; behind her, draperies form a kind of frame, and I have already suggested that at some point the image was concealed by curtains and only open to view at certain times. The seal itself can be dated as late twelfth/early thirteenth century.

In 1875 the Pynson Ballad (telling of the Shrine's foundation and discovered in the library of Magdelen College, Cambridge) was printed privately. It was no doubt this ballad's publication which gave rise to the two earliest English post-Reformation shrines to our Lady of Walsingham; one in the Anglican parish of Buxted in 1887 where the Lady Chapel was built to the dimensions of the holy house as given in the ballad, and one in the Roman Catholic Church at King's Lynn in 1897 (in which parish the Roman Catholics of the Walsingham area were incorporated) where the Lady Chapel contained a holy house, replica of the *casa sancta* of Loreto. But in neither of these places was there a copy of the original statue as shown on the Walsingham seal.

Meanwhile in 1894 Miss Charlotte Boyd, an ardent Anglo-Catholic who had installed some Anglican nuns following the Rule of St Benedict in her home at Malling Abbey, was looking for a new house for them. Her sights seem to have been set on the former priory, but en route to Walsingham village she happened upon what looked like a little chapel in a complex of barn and residence. Pausing to enquire she discovered this had once been the Slipper Chapel, last of the chapels en route to Walsingham, where pilgrims had removed their shoes before walking the last mile into England's Nazareth in bare feet. Immediately she set in motion plans for the chapel's purchase. However, before the legalities were finalised, Miss Boyd was received into the Catholic Church. At her own expense she arranged for the chapel to be separated from the buildings that had abutted it and for the exterior to be beautifully restored. She then wanted to give it to the Roman Catholic Diocese of Northampton but the bishop was not interested. 'There are no Catholics in Walsingham' was his excuse as he refused the gift. So Miss Boyd deeded the Chapel to the Benedictines of Downside. The bishop countered by forbidding services to be held there: the monks could only keep the chapel in good repair until some future, more auspicious time!

Fortunately Miss Boyd had the happiness of being part of the first ever pilgrimage to Walsingham since the Reformation which took place on August 20th 1897, the day following the inauguration of the holy house at King's Lynn. But she did not live to see the Slipper Chapel become the National Catholic Shrine as happened in later years. During her lifetime it remained beautifully clean, but empty and solitary, awaiting further developments.

Gradually interest in Walsingham was rekindled and in 1904 three windows were installed in the newly built Catholic church of St John the Baptist in Norwich, which told the story of Walsingham as far as it was then known. This church, founded by the same Duke of Norfolk who built the church dedicated to St Philip Howard in Arundel, has since become the seat of the Roman Catholic diocese of East Anglia, while the Church at Arundel is also now a cathedral. As the Catholic population of the area increased, a small church was opened at Fakenham, which incorporated Walsingham parish and showed a stained glass image of our Lady as depicted on the priory seal – its first reproduction in a religious setting. But there was still no movement to restore the pilgrimages of old.

Parallel to these developments, the Anglo-Catholic revival had reached Walsingham under the Revd Dr George Woodward who was appointed to the living of St Mary's (on the site of the former Church of All Saints mentioned by Geoffrey de Favarches in his Charter), from 1882–89. His successors continued in like vein until in 1921 the living once more fell vacant. This time a young priest who had known Buxted and very much wanted to restore an ancient shrine of our Lady in England, was offered the incumbency. His name was Alfred Hope Patten, and with him a new era in Walsingham's history began.

Fr Alfred Hope Patten came to Walsingham with the express intention of restoring devotion to our Lady of Walsingham in her own village. He was a man strongly Catholic in his sympathies; he was blessed with a touch of genius, plenty of imagination, and the gift of inspiring others with his own enthusiasm. He knew how to get the best from people – provided he himself remained firmly at the helm! He immediately set about having a statue carved from the priory seal, the first since the destruction of the original, and on July 6th 1922 he installed the image in the Guilds Chapel of St Mary's parish church, facing the site of the old priory. There the parish-ioners would gather daily at six o'clock to pray the rosary and offer intercessions – a custom continued down to the present day in the shrine church.

Word of the devotion spread and soon a trickle of pilgrims from Anglo-Catholic parishes began to arrive on pilgrimage. Numbers mushroomed and overnight accommodation was required. It occurred to Fr Hope Patten that a community of sisters would be a help in providing facilities for this and a group came from the sisters of St Peter Horbury near Wakefield. Alas, they did not long survive. Fr Hope Patten felt that he should govern them as their superior which was not satisfactory – they had their *own* superior.

Still Fr Hope Patten forged ahead with plans and projects. The living of Walsingham was in private gift and this worried him; a successor may well choose not to continue the work begun with such zeal. So it was decided to purchase a site and build a replica of the holy house in a special shrine church independent of the parish. Land was procured and work begun in 1931. Excavations on the site revealed remains of a cobbled courtyard and a well blocked with rubble and old leather soles. Mistakenly, Fr Hope Patten thought he had discovered the original site of the holy house and his enthusiasm doubled. The well was unblocked and has ever since been used as a source of water at the shrine for healing and blessing. A house was built to the proportions of Richeldis' chapel – but in brick and stone rather than wood, and the statue of our Lady was borne there in solemn procession on October 15th, feast of St Teresa of Avila the great Carmelite reformer. It would have been before similar statues that she herself must have prayed in her own day, as the Anglican Mother and Child are robed richly in the Spanish style beloved of Mediterranean peoples. It was a time of rejoicing for the whole village which turned out en fete for a day to remember. Round the holy house the shrine church was gradually enlarged and decorated – it is a real 'people's church' adorned with carvings and murals executed by local men and women as well as precious gifts sent from Anglican groups and congregations all over the world.

While the new Anglican shrine was in preparation and pilgrimages growing in number, the Slipper Chapel continued to stand empty. But in 1930 a new bishop was appointed to the Northampton Diocese, bishop Laurence Youens, and he determined that the Slipper Chapel should become the national Roman Catholic shrine of our Lady of Walsingham rather than King's Lynn. He saw to it that the chapel was refurbished and decorated interiorly in medieval English style and another statue was carved from the image on the priory seal and installed under a canopy.

By 1934 preparations were completed, and on August 19th Cardinal Bourne of Westminster led a pilgrimage of thousands to the Slipper Chapel after celebrating High Mass at St John's, Norwich. A priest custodian was assigned and in 1938 a chapel of the Holy Spirit was added, together with sacristies and a small cloister.

From this time both shrines have prospered, but not without a certain unfortunate rivalry in the early days.

After a number of vicissitudes Fr Hope Patten managed to obtain sisters of St Margaret from Haggeston Priory in London to care for the Anglican pilgrims; he also established a residence for priests to serve the shrine, although they have not evolved into a religious community as he had hoped. The Catholic shrine was served at first by secular priests, then for a while some Capuchin Franciscans came to the village. At present, priests and sisters of the Society of Mary (Marists) administer the Slipper Chapel, the Catholic Church of the Annunciation in the village and the new chapel of Reconciliation, erected beside the Slipper Chapel in 1982. Built in the style of a Norfolk barn, the latter is prayerful, uncluttered and able to accommodate large groups of worshippers.

It was the Second Vatican Council that opened the way for better ecumenical relationships. Now the staff and Directors of both shrines meet and worship together on a regular basis. In fact, the village is becoming more like one Shrine-Village with two focal points. Are we not in any case children of the same mother, brothers and sisters of her Son through our common Baptism? The priory grounds have remained in private hands. No one church has exclusive access to them, and it seems right that major pilgrimages, both Catholic and Anglican can enter the grounds and, under the ruins of the great East Window still standing, celebrate the Eucharist and pray on the site of the original holy house. At the Eucharist the focus is always Christ; Mary points to him just as she bears him for the world's salvation. May he one day 'make us one', which is his dearest desire. Mary has come back to Walsingham bringing her Child with her, and her presence is felt once more in the village of her choice.

In Walsingham today the mystery of the Incarnation again becomes a reality as the Angelus bell rings out in memory of the Angelic Salutation. Here Nazareth is recalled and the sanctity of family life upheld. Here in silent prayer and public praise pilgrims can experience love and acceptance, healing and wholeness. Above all they are summoned to rejoice with Mary and echo her 'yes' in their own lives – that in them too the Word may become flesh and dwell in today's world through their presence.

There are many beautiful incidents that could be recalled and mentioned, but the most evocative for me is the picture of Cardinal Hinsley in 1938 laying a sheaf of lilies silently at the place where once our Lady has asked for a little house to be built in memory of her 'root joy'. Only in silence can we rightly contemplate Mary and only in silent homage enter with her into the mystery of Nazareth.

> O gracious lady, glory of Jerusalem,
> Cypress of Sion and joy of Israel,
> Rose of Jericho and Star of Bethlehem.
> O glorious lady our requests ne'er repel.
> in mercy all other women you excel.
> Therefore blessed lady grant your great grace,
> to all who visit you devoutly in this place.
>
> (Pynson Ballad)

NOTES

1. Quoted on p. 305 *Our Lady's Dowry* by T. E. Bridgett. Burns and Oates 1875.
2. H. V. Morton *In Search of England*. Methuen & Co. 1927. M. R. James *Suffolk and Norfolk*. J. M. Dent & Sons 1930.

Index

93